coast

Australian chefs and their fearless way with food are taking the world by storm. In *Coast*, a stellar gathering of Australia's most accomplished chefs have contributed recipes that draw their inspiration from our coastal lifestyles and the diverse culinary cultures of the Asia–Pacific, Europe and the Americas.

With stunning photos taken on location along Australia's pristine shores, this timely and beautiful book celebrates a cuisine widely acknowledged to be among the most innovative in the world.

An experienced food journalist and restaurant reviewer, Kendall Hill is the travel editor of the *Sydney Morning Herald* and a former editor of 'Good Living', the *Herald*'s award-winning food and wine section. He writes for the *Sydney Morning Herald Good Food Guide* and has edited their *Café & Bar Guide*, as well as *The Age Cheap Eats* guide. Prior to this, he was in the hospitality industry for seven years, working at such Melbourne landmarks as Toofey's and Café La.

Jennifer Soo is a staff photographer at the *Sydney Morning Herald*, where her outstanding food photography appears in the pages of 'Good Living' each week. In 2001 she photographed Donna Hay's creations; now she works alongside chef Luke Mangan, co-owner of Sydney restaurants Salt and Bistro Lulu.

coast

seaside recipes from Australia's leading chefs

edited by Kendall Hill   with photography by Jennifer Soo

VIKING
an imprint of
PENGUIN BOOKS

Viking

Published by the Penguin Group
Penguin Books Australia Ltd
250 Camberwell Road, Camberwell, Victoria 3124, Australia
Penguin Books Ltd
80 Strand, London WC2R 0RL, England
Penguin Putnam Inc.
375 Hudson Street, New York, New York 10014, USA
Penguin Books Canada Limited
10 Alcorn Avenue, Toronto, Ontario, Canada M4V 3B2
Penguin Books (NZ) Ltd
Cnr Rosedale and Airborne Roads, Albany, Auckland, New Zealand
Penguin Books (South Africa) (Pty) Ltd
24 Sturdee Avenue, Rosebank, Johannesburg 2196, South Africa
Penguin Books India (P) Ltd
11, Community Centre, Panchsheel Park, New Delhi 110 017, India

First published by Penguin Books Australia Ltd 2003

10 9 8 7 6 5 4 3 2 1

Designed by Louise Leffler, Penguin Design Studio
Food styling and props by Ross Dobson
Typeset in Fairfield and Frutiger by Post Pre-press Group, Brisbane, Queensland
Colour reproduction by Splitting Image, Clayton, Victoria
Printed and bound in Singapore by Imago Productions

National Library of Australia
Cataloguing-in-Publication data:

Coast : seaside recipes from Australia's leading chefs.

Includes index.
ISBN 0 670 04086 X.

1. Cookery. 2. Desserts. I. Hill, Kendall. II. Soo, Jennifer.

641.5

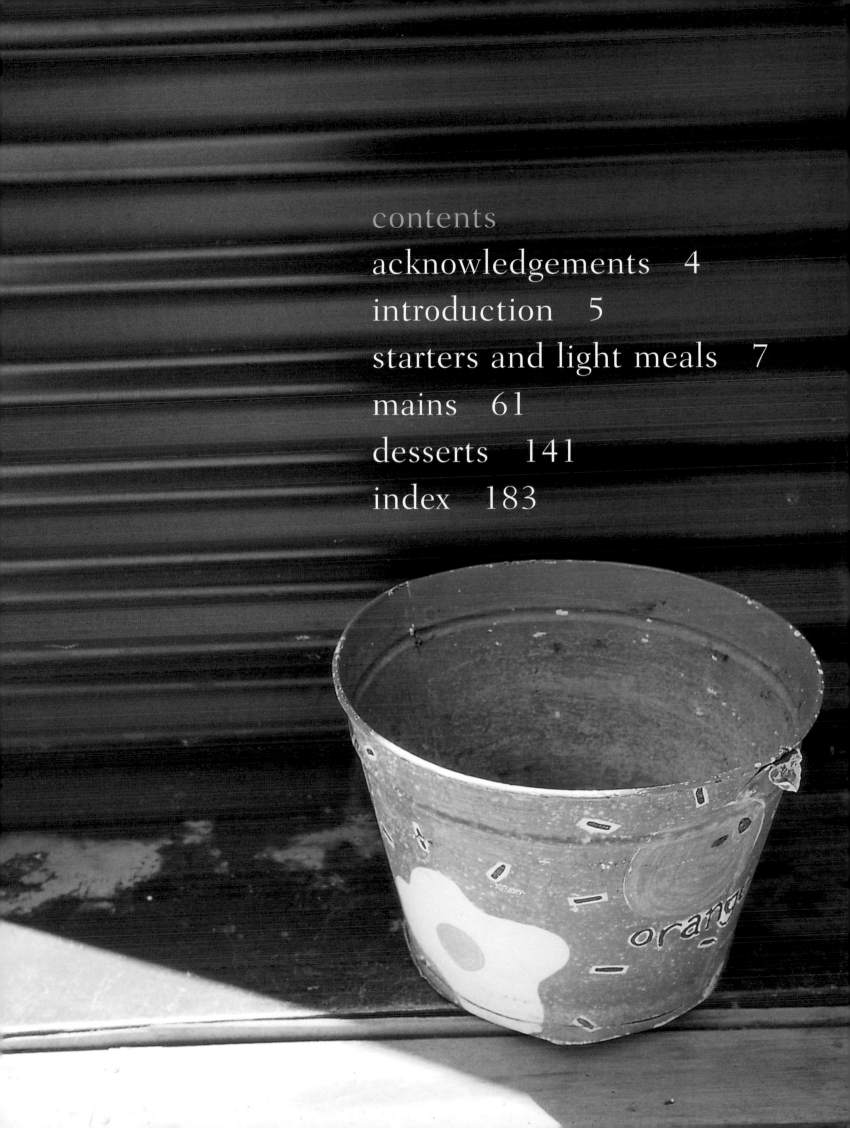

contents

Busselton, Western Australia

Hobart, Tasmania

acknowledgements

Firstly, thank you to the chefs who contributed so generously, sharing their recipes with food lovers everywhere. They are the stars of *Coast*.

Thank you also to:

Jennifer Soo, for her gorgeous photography and her companionship on the road.

Ross Dobson, for his wonderful styling and his good humour.

Alison Cowan, senior editor at Penguin, for her patient, assiduous commitment to this project, and senior designer Louise Leffler for her beautiful layout – and to both of you for your eager involvement and encouragement.

Executive publisher Julie Gibbs for enthusiastic support (and faith).

Bill Tikos for making this happen.

Virgin Blue and Quest apartments for looking after us admirably during our national photography tour – except on the Fleurieu Peninsula, where Fergus and Karen Simpson, and John, Zanni, Dustin and co at the Star of Greece Café, showed us real South Australian hospitality.

My mum, Audrey Richards, for her loving support – especially for being the self-described 'general dogsbody' during the food shoots.

Brett Galvin, and all my friends subjected to endless experimental dinner parties, for many delicious moments.

introduction

More than four out of every five Australians live by the sea, and our lifestyles are tempered by the oceans – the way we work, the way we relax, the way we eat. Especially the way we eat. Of course, seafood features prominently, but so does fresh, seasonal produce from the hinterland. Peer inside an Australian kitchen and you will find ingredients as varied as pasta, saffron, lemongrass, feta, pide, fish sauce, pappadums, couscous and wasabi. For our food, like our population, draws its character from around the world, and the result is an exciting, innovative cuisine widely admired across the globe.

Coast is a celebration of that cuisine. Over a hundred of the country's finest chefs, their backgrounds ranging from French, Italian, Greek, Spanish and Turkish to Chinese, Malaysian, Cambodian and Indian, have contributed recipes that capture the essence of Australia – fresh, often surprising, but always down to earth.

This is real food for real people: impromptu suppers with friends, impressive meals for special occasions, food for carefree summer days or chilly winter nights. Many of the dishes are light and simple, reflecting how much we prize time – try Tetsuya Wakuda's tartare of tuna with goat's cheese, Steven Snow's piri piri prawns or Neil Perry's steamed Pacific oysters with mirin and soy. Others, such as Teage Ezard's seaweed and dashi-salted yellowfin tuna with wasabi and sour cream mash, will challenge you, then delight you with the results.

What all the recipes have in common, however, is that they reflect the philosophy of Australian dining today. We like to eat exceptionally well; we like to experiment, but we don't like too much fuss; and, most of all, we like to share.

Australia, the lucky country? See for yourself.

Busselton, Western Australia

starters and light meals

ma hor ('galloping horse') of minced duck, peanuts, seared scallops and pineapple

David Coomer, Star Anise

This dish works well as a canape (the quantities here will serve 16 people), as a light starter, or as one course of a Thai banquet. For the minced duck, I steam duck necks for about 1½ hours, then shred the meat from them – this produces a succulent and flavoursome 'mince'.

Heat 2 tablespoons of peanut oil in a wok over medium heat. Stir-fry garlic, coriander root, chilli and pepper until they are fragrant and the garlic is golden. Add duck meat and fry for 4 minutes, or until it is well sealed, stirring occasionally to prevent the meat clumping together. Add palm sugar and fish sauce and cook until well caramelised – the mixture is ready when it's dark golden in colour and is beginning to smell of caramel rather than sugar. Add peanuts, half the coriander leaves and the lime juice. Mix well and keep warm.

Deep-fry the shallots until lightly golden, then drain on kitchen paper.

Lay the pineapple slices on four plates: narrow sushi plates look good, or use one large platter. Place a spoonful of the duck mixture on each slice of pineapple.

Pour a little peanut or vegetable oil onto a hot chargrill plate or non-stick frying pan, lightly sear the scallops (about 25–30 seconds each side) and place one on each 'ma hor'. Garnish with the deep-fried shallots and the remaining chopped coriander leaves, then serve.

David Coomer worked at the former Merivale restaurant and at the Regent Hotel in Sydney before moving to Perth in 1991. He opened the Asian-inspired Star Anise – where he is 'proprietor, head cook and dishwasher' – in 1998.
Star Anise, 225 Onslow Road, Shenton Park, Western Australia 6008 (08 9381 9811)

SERVES 4

peanut oil for frying
3 cloves garlic, finely chopped
4 coriander roots, finely chopped
1 long red chilli, finely chopped
¼ teaspoon ground white pepper
375 g (12 oz) minced duck meat
75 g (2½ oz) palm sugar, dissolved
   in a little warm water
2 tablespoons fish sauce
75 g (2½ oz) roasted peanuts,
   coarsely chopped
2 tablespoons coriander (cilantro)
   leaves, chopped
juice of 2 limes
2 golden shallots, shaved with
   a mandoline or finely sliced
16 slices fresh pineapple
16 sea scallops

rice paper roll of beef tartare and marinated mushrooms

Marc Romanella, Boomerang

SERVES 2–4

375 g (12 oz) assorted mushrooms
3 tablespoons soy sauce
3 tablespoons port
2 teaspoons finely chopped ginger
2 teaspoons finely chopped chilli
1½ tablespoons lime juice
375 g (12 oz) beef tenderloin
salt and pepper
1½ teaspoons truffle oil
1 packet rice paper wrappers
handful of fresh mizuna leaves

DRESSING
1 teaspoon fish sauce
1 teaspoon palm sugar
1 tablespoon light soy sauce
1 teaspoon lime juice
½ teaspoon finely chopped chilli

This dish is a head-on collision between French and Asian cooking – it is delicate yet powerful, subtle yet simple.

Sauté mushrooms until browned then add soy sauce, port, ginger, chilli and lime and reduce over a medium heat for 5 minutes. Remove from heat and process the mixture coarsely in a blender or food processor. Finely chop beef and season with salt, pepper and truffle oil. Combine beef and mushrooms.

Soak rice paper wrappers in hot water for 10 seconds and lay out on a flat surface. Place 1½ tablespoons of the beef and mushroom mixture in the centre of each rice paper wrapper, then roll up like a spring roll.

Combine dressing ingredients and toss through the mizuna.

Cut the rolls in half diagonally, arrange mizuna in between the rolls, and serve.

Australian-born **Marc Romanella** trained in Canada, learned the secrets of Asian cooking while working as a head chef in Beijing, returned to Canada to study French cuisine, then came home to open Boomerang with his brother Paul. **Boomerang**, 14 Middleton Street, Byron Bay, New South Wales 2481 (02 6685 5707)

Byron Bay, New South Wales

ella's wrap

Simon Goh, Chinta Ria Temple of Love

Ella's wrap, named for Ella Fitzgerald, makes very snappy finger food. You can jive with it.

Place onion, garlic, chilli, turmeric, lemongrass, lime leaf, salt and sugar in blender and process to a fine paste. Heat 1–2 tablespoons of oil in a frying pan and cook the paste for a few minutes, until fragrant. Set aside to cool.

Cut a spring-roll wrapper diagonally in half, then cut one of the halves in half again to make two smaller triangles. Place one of the smaller triangles in the middle of the larger one.

Make an incision in the back of each of the prawns and fill it with some of the paste. Place a stuffed prawn onto the wrapper, with its tail sticking out of the bottom. Fold down the point of the triangle then wrap around into a spring-roll shape, sealing the flap with cornflour paste. Continue until all the prawns are wrapped.

Heat oil in a pan or wok and deep-fry the wraps for 2–3 minutes, or until golden brown. Put the wraps on kitchen paper to absorb excess oil, then serve with lemon wedges.

Simon Goh made Malaysian hawker-style food funky with his Chinta Ria restaurants – first in Melbourne, then at the Temple of Love in Sydney. Born in Malaysia, he began his food career as a kitchen hand at the world's most famous burger chain.

Chinta Ria Temple of Love, The Roof Terrace, Cockle Bay Wharf at Darling Park, 201 Sussex Street, Sydney, New South Wales 2000 (02 9264 3211)

SERVES 4 (MAKES 12 WRAPS)

1 onion, chopped

2 cloves garlic, chopped

4 dried red chillies, soaked, drained and chopped

1 teaspoon ground turmeric

1 stalk lemongrass, white part only, chopped

1 lime leaf, finely shredded

1 teaspoon salt

1 teaspoon sugar

vegetable oil for frying

12 spring-roll wrappers

12 uncooked prawns (shrimp), peeled and deveined but with tails left on

1 teaspoon cornflour (cornstarch) mixed with 1 tablespoon cold water

2 lemons, cut into wedges

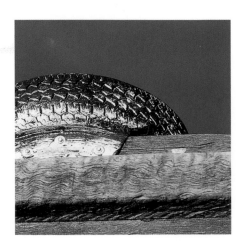

simple salmon with cucumber and asparagus

Neal Jackson, Jackson's Restaurant

SERVES 4

30 ml (1 fl oz) sherry vinegar
salt and pepper
100 ml (3 fl oz) extra virgin olive oil
1 tomato, peeled and diced
1 red onion, peeled and diced
1 orange, peeled and diced, seeds removed
4 basil leaves, torn
250 g (8 oz) fresh asparagus
1 cucumber, cut into spaghetti-like strips
a little olive oil
500 g (1 lb) fresh salmon, cut into 5 mm
   (¼ in) slices

This is very simple to prepare – it takes just seconds under the grill, and you can have it all ready to go before your guests arrive.

First make the dressing by pouring the vinegar into a bowl and stirring in some salt and pepper to taste. When dissolved, whisk in the oil, then add the tomato, onion, orange and basil.

Put a steamer or large pan of salted water on the stove and bring to the boil. Steam or poach the asparagus for 1 minute. When it is almost cooked, add the cucumber strips to the pan, then drain. Toss the asparagus and cucumber with a little of the dressing.

Brush four heatproof plates with olive oil. Place about four slices of salmon on each plate in a single layer, and season with salt and pepper. Place the plates of salmon in a hot oven – 230°C (450°F) – or under a grill for 1–2 minutes. Garnish each plate with the asparagus and cucumber, and drizzle some more dressing over the lot.

Nottingham-born **Neal Jackson** did his apprenticeship at London's Savoy Hotel and came to Perth in 1971. He has gained major food awards for a succession of West Australian restaurants. He opened Jackson's Restaurant in 1998, and credits cooking tours to Japan, Hong Kong and Indonesia with influencing his food today.
Jackson's Restaurant, 483 Beaufort Street, Highgate, Western Australia 6003
(08 9328 1177); www.jacksonsrestaurant.com.au

Cottesloe, Western Australia

pan-seared calamari with chilli, tomato, basil and risotto cake

Karen Martini, Melbourne Wine Room / Icebergs Dining Room and Bar

First make the risotto cake. Preheat oven to 170°C (340°F). Bring 6 cups of water to the boil. In a medium-sized, heavy-based pan, fry the onion, garlic and bay leaf in a little olive oil until the onion is translucent, then add the rice and fry until it is hot to the touch. Start adding the boiling water, a ladleful at a time, to the pan. Add the salt and continue adding the water until it is absorbed – about 15 minutes. Add the flour, stirring constantly. Keep adding water until the rice is sticky and almost cooked.

Spread out a 50 cm (20 in) length of foil, cover with non-stick baking paper and spoon rice along one edge. Roll up paper and foil to make a log 6–8 cm (2–3 in) fat. Tie the ends like a bonbon and place in a baking dish with the seam side facing up. Add 2 cups of boiling water to the dish and cook the risotto cake in the oven for 25–30 minutes, until firm. Remove and chill in fridge for at least 3 hours.

Meanwhile, make the pea paste. Bring 2 cups of water to the boil, season with salt and pepper and the sugar. Add the peas and cook for 5 minutes. Strain, reserving the liquid. Place the peas in a blender, add half the oil and the reserved cooking liquid, then purée until smooth. Add the remaining oil and adjust seasoning.

Split the calamari tubes and remove and reserve tentacles. Place the blade of a large cook's knife down at an angle on the calamari tubes and slice off long, very thin strips. Divide the tentacles into pairs, discarding any long ones. Heat a very large non-stick frying pan until it is very hot. Add a splash of oil and quickly sear the calamari in batches, so as not to crowd the pan – it should only take about 2 minutes for each batch. When all the calamari is seared, return it to the pan, add the chilli, garlic, basil and ground coriander, then fry until fragrant – about 1 minute. Add the tomato sauce and vinaigrette, and stir gently until heated through. Adjust seasoning to taste, then keep warm.

To serve, cut slices of the risotto cake about 1 cm (½ in) thick and fry in hot oil until golden brown. Dab a little pea paste on each plate, cover with a risotto cake and a little more pea paste. Top with the witlof, watercress and calamari, then drizzle over a little lemon juice.

Karen Martini began her career at Tansy's in Melbourne, became executive chef and a partner at Melbourne Wine Room, and last year was appointed executive chef at the Icebergs Dining Room and Bar in Bondi.

Melbourne Wine Room, 125 Fitzroy Street, St Kilda, Victoria 3182 (03 9525 5599)

Icebergs Dining Room and Bar, Notts Avenue, Bondi Beach, New South Wales 2026 (02 9130 3120)

SERVES 4–6

2 medium calamari, 625 g (1¼ lb)
  in total, cleaned
olive oil for frying
4 small red chillies, finely chopped
4 cloves garlic
12 basil leaves, torn
1 tablespoon ground roasted coriander seeds
¾ cup homemade tomato sauce or
  good-quality bottled pasta sauce
60 ml (2 fl oz) French vinaigrette
salt and pepper
1 head witlof (Belgian endive),
  cut into fine strips
2 handfuls watercress, picked
1 lemon

RISOTTO CAKE

¼ brown onion, finely diced
1 clove garlic, finely diced
½ bay leaf – preferably fresh
olive oil for frying
250 g (8 oz) arborio rice
½ teaspoon salt
2 tablespoons plain (all-purpose) flour

PEA PASTE

salt and pepper
½ teaspoon sugar
250 g (8 oz) frozen peas
100 ml (3 fl oz) extra virgin olive oil

basil-infused tuna with soy vinaigrette

Guillaume Brahimi, Guillaume at Bennelong

I created this dish when I arrived in Australia 10 years ago because I was so impressed with the quality of Australian tuna. I'd recommend pairing it with a glass of Cullen's semillon sauvignon blanc.

Divide tuna into four steaks of equal size. Pick basil leaves from stalks, blanch in boiling water then plunge into icy water. Season tuna steaks with salt and pepper then wrap each one in basil leaves.

Make a vinaigrette by combining the olive oil, soy sauce and mustard seeds, adding lime juice to taste.

Steam tuna for 45 seconds (the tuna should be warm but not cooked), then cut each piece in half on an angle. Brush with vinaigrette and serve on a bed of mixed leaves.

Paris-born **Guillaume Brahimi** gained his Michelin three-star experience at La Tour D'Argent and Jamin in his home city. His success followed him to Sydney, where his restaurants Pond, Quay and Guillaume at Bennelong have garnered many major awards.

Guillaume at Bennelong, Sydney Opera House, Bennelong Point, Sydney, New South Wales 2000 (02 9241 1999); www.guillaumeatbennelong.com.au

SERVES 4

250 g (8 oz) sashimi-quality tuna,
   in one piece
1 bunch basil
salt and pepper
2 tablespoons extra virgin olive oil
2 teaspoons soy sauce
2 teaspoons mustard seeds
juice of 1 lime
mixed salad leaves, to serve

Noosa River, Queensland

potato gnocchi with spanner crab, broad beans and crispy shallots

Matt Golinski, Ricky Ricardo's

SERVES 6

2 kg (4 lb) broad (fava) beans, shelled
1 kg (2 lb) potato gnocchi
6 large golden shallots, finely sliced
vegetable oil for frying
1 onion, finely diced
1 clove garlic, sliced
2 tablespoons olive oil
1–1½ cups vegetable stock
1 cup cream
500 g (1 lb) picked spanner crab meat
4 tablespoons finely grated parmesan
salt and ground white pepper

This is a delicious and simple starter for summer. Make sure the sauce is fairly thin and creamy; if it becomes gluggy, thin it with a little more vegetable stock.

Blanch the shelled broad beans in salted boiling water for 2–3 minutes, drain and plunge into iced water. When cool, remove skins.

Add gnocchi to plenty of salted boiling water a few at a time and, as they rise to the surface, remove and drop into iced water.

Fry the shallots in 1 cm (½ in) of vegetable oil over medium heat until golden. Spread onto kitchen paper and leave in a warm place so they stay crispy.

In a large pan, sauté the onion and garlic in the olive oil until transparent. Add 1 cup of the vegetable stock and bring to the boil. Add the cream and simmer until reduced by half. Turn the heat down to a slow simmer, and flake in the crab meat. Add the broad beans and parmesan, and season with salt and white pepper. Simmer gently until everything is heated through.

Plunge the gnocchi into boiling water for 1 minute, then strain and add to the crab mixture. If necessary, thin the sauce with a little more vegetable stock and check the seasoning. Divide between six bowls and garnish with the fried shallots.

Matt Golinski was born and bred on the Sunshine Coast. He did his training at Chevaliers Restaurant in Brisbane, toured Australia and abroad gathering food ideas, and has been the chef at Ricky Ricardo's since 1999.
Ricky Ricardo's, Noosa Wharf, Quamby Place, Noosa Heads, Queensland 4567 (07 5447 2455)

fiori di zucca ripieni (stuffed zucchini flowers)

Salvatore Pepe, Cibo Ristorante

This is a southern Italian recipe traditionally made with buffalo mozzarella and anchovies, but I prefer the flavours of ricotta and mushrooms.

First make the *pastella*, or batter. Put the yeast and flour in a bowl, then add the water, mixing for a minute until the batter has a glue-like consistency (add more water if required). Cover with cling film and let rest for 30 minutes in a warm place.

Soak the porcini in hot water for 20 minutes, then strain and chop into small pieces. Fry the onion in the tablespoon of olive oil until golden, then add the porcini and cook for a further 5 minutes. Remove from the heat and place in a bowl with the ricotta and thyme. Mix well, seasoning with salt and pepper if desired.

Carefully open the petals of the zucchini flowers and spoon or pipe in a walnut-sized amount of the ricotta mixture. Dip the flowers in the batter, coating them very well. In a pan or wok, heat the 2 cups of oil until there's a slight haze just above the surface, then fry the flowers for 2–3 minutes each side until they are a nice golden colour.

Place the cooked flowers on kitchen paper to drain excess oil. Sprinkle with salt and serve immediately.

Salvatore Pepe was born in Calabria and began his career working as a waiter in Florence, but his passion for food eventually led him to the kitchen. Five years later, at the age of 26, he moved to Sydney, where he worked with Armando Percuoco at Buon Ricordo. He has been co-proprietor and chef at Cibo Ristorante, in Adelaide, since 1996.

Cibo Ristorante, 8 O'Connell Street, North Adelaide, South Australia 5006 (08 8267 2444)

SERVES 4

30 g (1 oz) fresh yeast *or* 15 g (½ oz)
   dry yeast
400 g (13 oz) plain (all-purpose) flour
400 ml (13 fl oz) warm water –
   about 40°C (100°F)
30 g (1 oz) dried porcini mushrooms
1 tablespoon diced onion
1 tablespoon olive oil
200 g (6 oz) fresh ricotta cheese
pinch thyme leaves
salt and pepper
8 zucchini (courgette) flowers, fruit attached
2 cups olive or vegetable oil

smoked cod, salmon, scallop and potato soup

Michael Wood, Pier Nine

This recipe is an adaptation of a very popular Scottish fish soup, Cullen Skink ('skink' is an old Scots word for broth). It originated from the picturesque fishing village of Cullen on the Banffshire coast. This is my version, which we serve at Pier Nine.

Preheat oven to very low – about 80°C (175°F).

Butter a large casserole dish big enough to hold the cod fillets. Place fillets in dish and cover with milk. Poach gently in oven, without allowing milk to boil, for 8–10 minutes or until fish has softened. This will infuse the milk with the smoky flavour of the cod. Remove from oven and, when cool enough to handle, take fish from milk and discard skin and bones. Roughly flake fish, place in a bowl and set aside. Reserve milk.

In a large saucepan, melt butter and sweat onion until soft. Add diced potato, cook slowly for a couple of minutes, then add fish stock. Add parsley, smoked salmon and bay leaves and season with salt and pepper. Simmer until potato is almost cooked, then pour in reserved milk. Add flaked fish, check seasoning again, and add a little cream if desired – the soup should be quite thick.

Lightly score a crisscross pattern on each side of scallops. Pour a little oil into a hot frying pan and sear scallops for about 25 seconds on each side (scallops are best served rare).

To serve, ladle the soup into four bowls and place three scallops on top of each. Decorate with sprigs of chervil.

Michael Wood was born and bred in Edinburgh. He started his apprenticeship there at the renowned Prestonfield Hotel in 1974, and came to Australia to live in 1985. He has been executive chef at Brisbane's Pier Nine since 1994.
Pier Nine, Eagle Street Pier, Queensland 4001 (07 3229 2194); www.piernine.com.au

SERVES 4

2 large fillets of smoked cod –
    each about 500 g (1 lb)
3 cups milk
300 g (10 oz) butter
2 onions, finely chopped
4 large potatoes, roughly diced
8 cups fish stock
1 cup curly-leaf parsley, chopped
250 g (8 oz) smoked salmon, finely chopped
2 bay leaves
sea salt and freshly ground black pepper
a little cream – optional
12 large sea scallops, roe removed
olive oil for frying
a few sprigs of fresh chervil

prawns with salsa fresca

Brian Jackson, Jackson's

SERVES 4

splash of olive oil
16 large uncooked tiger prawns (shrimp),
    peeled and deveined but with
    tails left intact
1 clove garlic, crushed
1 tablespoon dry white wine
1 tablespoon lemon juice
knob of butter
sea salt and freshly ground black pepper
1½ cups rocket (arugula),
    washed and drained well
1½ cups baby spinach leaves,
    washed and drained well
1 lemon, cut into wedges

SALSA

½ red onion, finely diced
1 large ripe but firm avocado,
    chopped into 5 mm (¼ in) dice
⅓ large cucumber, seeded
    and finely chopped
4 roma (plum) tomatoes, seeded
    and finely chopped
1 tablespoon chopped parsley
1 tablespoon chopped coriander
    (cilantro) leaves
juice of ½ lime
1 tablespoon olive oil
1–3 fresh red or green chillies,
    finely chopped

This is a twist on the classic prawn and avocado combination – it's full of freshness and is best eaten al fresco.

In a bowl, gently mix all the salsa ingredients together. Season to taste with salt and pepper, and adjust lime juice or olive oil amounts if necessary. Set aside.

Heat a little olive oil in a heavy-based frying pan. When sizzling, seal the prawns. As the prawns begin to change colour, add the garlic, wine and lemon juice and simmer for a couple of minutes. Swirl in the knob of butter and quickly remove from the heat. (Don't let the garlic burn or the prawns overcook – the whole cooking process for the prawns should barely take 4–5 minutes.) Season to taste.

On each of four plates, or a serving platter, arrange a pile of rocket and spinach leaves. Mound the salsa in the middle and arrange four prawns per person around the salsa. Spoon a little of the pan juice over the prawns only, and serve with lemon wedges.

Brian Jackson arrived in Noosa from New Zealand 20 years ago and hasn't left the Sunshine Coast since. After working at a succession of the region's fine restaurants, he opened his own – Jackson's – in 1998.

Jackson's, 12 Thomas Street, Noosaville, Queensland 4566 (07 5474 0999)

vine-ripened tomato tart with raclette cheese and pesto

Javier Codina, Gianni Restaurant and Wine Bar

SERVES 4

4 sheets puff pastry
1 egg yolk
100 g (3 oz) raclette cheese
4 tablespoons sun-dried tomatoes
8 large roma (plum) tomatoes
4 tablespoons wholegrain mustard
salt and pepper

PESTO
100 g (3 oz) pine nuts
1 cup basil leaves
2 cloves garlic, halved
²/₃ cup extra virgin olive oil
salt and pepper

This is a very Mediterranean recipe – except for the Heidi raclette cheese, which is pure Tasmanian.

Cut the pastry into four rounds 13 cm (5 in) in diameter and place on a baking tray. For each base, also cut a strip of pastry 1 cm (¹/₂ in) wide and 13 cm (5 in) long and place around the edge of each base. Brush the pastry with a little egg yolk and set aside. Preheat the oven to 180°C (350°F).

Cut the cheese into four cubes. Purée the sun-dried tomatoes in a blender. Cut the roma tomatoes into slices about 1 cm (¹/₂ in) thick.

To make the pesto, place the pine nuts on a baking tray and toast in the oven for 5 minutes. Remove, but leave the oven on for the tarts. Place the pine nuts, basil, garlic and olive oil in a blender, or grind together with a mortar and pestle. Season with salt and pepper.

Spread each tart base with 1 tablespoon of wholegrain mustard and 1 tablespoon of sun-dried tomato purée. Place cheese cubes in the middle of the pastry bases and build the sliced tomatoes around (allow 7–9 slices per tart). Season with salt and pepper.

Place the tarts in the oven and bake for 15–20 minutes.

Serve the tarts hot, adding 1 teaspoon of pesto on top of each tart.

Javier Codina was born in Barcelona, where he began his career in the kitchen of the Newport Room at the Hotel Arts, before moving to San Francisco to work with Gary Danko, and to England to cook at the Chewton Glen Hotel. He came to Australia to take up the position of head chef at the Hayman Island Resort, and he is now executive chef at Gianni Restaurant and Wine Bar in Brisbane.

Gianni Restaurant and Wine Bar, 12 Edward Street, Brisbane, Queensland 4000 (07 3221 7655); www.giannisrestaurant.com

caesar salad soup with speck emulsion
Noriyuki Sugie

This soup has a very Australian sense of style. It's served warm, unlike a caesar salad, and makes a healthy start to lunch or dinner.

To make the soup, roughly chop the onion, celery, leek, garlic and thyme, then sauté in a large saucepan with a little oil until soft but not browned. Add the chicken stock and simmer for 30 minutes.

Meanwhile, make the emulsion. Brown the speck or bacon in a frying pan, then deglaze with the chicken stock. Simmer for 30 minutes then strain, keeping the liquid. Combine this with the cream and butter, adding salt and pepper to taste. (If you like, you can finely chop the speck or bacon and add it to the soup; otherwise, discard.)

In another pan, boil plenty of salted water and blanch the cos lettuce for 1 minute or until just tender. Strain through a colander and refresh in cold water.

Combine all the soup ingredients except the parmesan in a blender and purée, seasoning to taste with salt and pepper.

To serve, gently reheat the soup then pour into six demitasse cups or small bowls and spoon a layer of emulsion onto the surface of each. Finish with a sprinkle of grated parmesan.

Born in Japan, **Noriyuki Sugie** has worked in France with Michel Trama at the Michelin two-star restaurant Les Loges de l'Aubergade, in Chicago with the famed Charlie Trotter and, most recently, in Sydney at Restaurant VII.

SERVES 6

½ onion
1 stalk celery
½ leek
1 clove garlic
1 sprig thyme
vegetable oil for frying
4 cups chicken stock
1 cos lettuce, roughly chopped
salt and pepper
1 tablespoon grated parmesan

SPECK EMULSION
250 g (8 oz) speck or diced bacon
1 cup chicken stock
100 ml (3 fl oz) cream
2 knobs butter
salt and pepper

chilli-roasted vine-ripened tomatoes with piquillo peppers and fresh kervella goat's cheese

David Rayner, berardo's

This is a rough, rustic dish that makes for great eating with some fresh country-style bread, but all the ingredients must be in perfect condition – try to find some really ripe organic tomatoes. My favourite olive oil for this recipe is Australian-made Joseph's.

Preheat oven to 120°C (250°F).

Remove cores from tomatoes, then cut in half and squeeze gently to remove juice and pips. Arrange tomatoes on a baking tray or dish and cover liberally with garlic slivers, chilli and oregano. Dress with sea salt flakes and olive oil. Roast tomatoes for 20 minutes. Remove from oven, set aside and allow to cool.

When tomatoes have cooled, arrange on four plates or bowls with capers, basil, olives and peppers, then dress with balsamic vinegar.

Cut goat's cheese into small chunks, season with a pinch of sea salt and drizzle with olive oil then arrange on top of the tomatoes.

English-born **David Rayner** began his career at London's Savoy Hotel. He moved to Australia in 1994 and produced award-winning food at two Sydney restaurants – Lucciola in Balmain, and Vault in The Rocks – before relocating to berardo's on the Sunshine Coast in 2000.

berardo's, 49 Hastings Street, Noosa Heads, Queensland 4567 (07 5447 5666)

SERVES 4

1 kg (2 lb) vine-ripened tomatoes
2 cloves garlic, cut into thin slivers
1 long red chilli, sliced
1 tablespoon fresh oregano, roughly chopped
sea salt flakes
2 teaspoons extra virgin olive oil
1 tablespoon capers
18 leaves organic basil
2 tablespoons Ligurian olives
4 Spanish piquillo peppers, torn in half
   or 1 large chargrilled red capsicum
   (bell pepper), peeled and deseeded
2 teaspoons aged balsamic vinegar
75 g (2½ oz) fresh Kervella goat's cheese
   or any other good-quality goat's cheese
extra virgin olive oil for drizzling

master-stock quail breast with slow-cooked cuttlefish, prosciutto and shiitake mushrooms

Peter Gilmore, Quay

SERVES 4

4 large quails – each about 200 g (6 oz)
1 tablespoon sesame oil
250 g (8 oz) cleaned cuttlefish or squid
200 g (6 oz) fresh shiitake mushrooms,
    stalks removed
6 thin slices prosciutto
2 medium-sized spring onions
    (scallions), thinly sliced
2 teaspoons mirin
2 teaspoons salt-reduced soy sauce
pinch sea salt

MASTER STOCK
8 cups chicken stock
100 ml (3 fl oz) shaohsing
    Chinese cooking wine
100 ml (3 fl oz) dark soy sauce
125 g (4 oz) yellow rock sugar
6 star anise
3 strips cassia bark
4 strips dried orange peel
1 teaspoon Sichuan peppercorns

GARLIC OIL
2 cups olive oil
6 garlic cloves, cut in half

This is a Chinese method of poaching, which imparts a lovely flavour to the quail. Combined with slivers of slow-cooked cuttlefish, prosciutto and shiitake mushroom, the flavours harmonise and the textures meld into each other.

For the master stock, combine all the ingredients in a large stockpot, bring to the boil and simmer gently for 30 minutes. Remove from heat and leave to infuse for 1 hour. Strain and reserve stock. Make the garlic oil by warming olive oil in a pan with garlic for 5 minutes. Remove from heat and leave to infuse for 1 hour. Strain.

Bring the master stock back to the boil, then turn down to barely simmering. Remove the legs from the quails and reserve for another use. Brush quail breasts with sesame oil and poach in master stock for exactly 2 minutes. Remove quail breasts from stock and allow to cool. Take the meat off the bone, then carefully remove and discard the skin. Set aside the meat.

Place cuttlefish or squid on a board and, with a sharp knife, cut horizontally into paper-thin slivers. Carefully slice the shiitake mushroom caps into paper-thin slivers. Cut the prosciutto into 4 cm (1½ in) strips. Fry spring onions in a little garlic oil until just caramelised; drain on kitchen paper and set aside. Put the master stock back on the stove and heat to just below simmering point.

In a large saucepan, warm all except 1 tablespoon of the remaining garlic oil to 70°C (160°F). Submerge cuttlefish or squid slivers in oil for about 30 seconds. Remove with a slotted spoon as soon as they turn opaque. Set aside in a warmed bowl, season lightly with sea salt and toss through the prosciutto slices and spring onions. Sauté shiitake mushrooms in the reserved tablespoon of garlic oil until golden brown. Add mirin and salt-reduced soy sauce, simmer until slightly reduced, then add to cuttlefish or squid mixture and gently combine.

Poach quail breasts in master stock for 1 minute. Remove from stock and place two breasts in the middle of each of four warmed plates. Top with the cuttlefish or squid mixture, and serve immediately.

Sydney-born **Peter Gilmore** dashed off to London at the age of 18 to work at the prestigious Oak Room in Piccadilly, before returning home to cook in a succession of top-end restaurants. His latest venture, Quay, was named restaurant of the year in the *Sydney Morning Herald Good Food Guide 2003*.

Quay, Overseas Passenger Terminal, Circular Quay West, The Rocks, New South Wales 2000 (02 9251 5600); www.quay.com.au

grilled sea scallops with celeriac purée, tapenade and green apple sauce

Dietmar Sawyere, Forty One

Australia has fantastic seafood, and the large scallops from Queensland are one of my favourites, especially when combined as here with the saltiness of olives, the creaminess of celeriac and the tang of apple – a taste sensation in every mouthful, perfectly accompanied by a crisp riesling.

First make the tapenade: sauté the mushrooms in the tablespoon of olive oil until well cooked (about 5 minutes), then drain on kitchen paper. Blend together garlic, anchovies, capers and chilli powder in a food processor. Add mushrooms and pitted olives. Process slowly, gradually adding the extra virgin olive oil. Transfer the tapenade to a bowl, add parsley, and season to taste with lemon juice and pepper. Set aside.

Sweat shallots in a large saucepan with a little butter then add celeriac and potato. Cover with chicken stock and milk. Bring to the boil and simmer until celeriac and potato are cooked – about 15–20 minutes. Drain, reserving the stock, then purée the vegetables in a food processor. Keep the purée warm while you prepare the scallops and the sauce.

Pour apple juice and 2 tablespoons of the lemon juice into a non-reactive pan, bring to the boil and reduce to a syrupy consistency – about 15 minutes.

Brush scallops with melted butter and place on a very hot chargrill. Grill for 30 seconds, then rotate scallops at right angles. Leave for another 30 seconds, then turn over and repeat the process. Remove scallops from grill and drizzle the remaining lemon juice over them. Season with seaweed salt, if you have it, or sea salt, and a grinding of white pepper.

Place three separate teaspoonfuls of celeriac purée on a plate and place a seared scallop on top of each. Place a small dollop of tapenade in the centre of the plate. Drizzle the scallops and tapenade with the green apple sauce. Sprinkle the chives on each of the scallops, and place a sprig of chervil on the tapenade.

Swiss-born **Dietmar Sawyere**'s career began at 16, in the kitchens of London's Savoy Hotel. A former young chef of the year in London, and chef of the year (twice) in New Zealand, he has operated the award-wining Forty One restaurant since 1983.

Forty One, Chifley Tower, 2 Chifley Square, Sydney, New South Wales 2000 (02 9221 2500); www.forty-one.com.au

SERVES 6

10 golden shallots, roughly chopped
a little softened butter
2 large celeriac, peeled and roughly chopped
3 large potatoes, peeled and roughly chopped
3/4 cup chicken stock
100 ml (3 fl oz) milk
300 ml (10 fl oz) apple juice
3 tablespoons lemon juice
18 sea scallops, roe off
a little melted butter
Japanese seaweed salt *or* sea salt
freshly ground white pepper
1 tablespoon finely chopped chives
6 chervil sprigs

TAPENADE

125 g (4 oz) field mushrooms, sliced
1 tablespoon olive oil
1 garlic clove, sliced
2 anchovy fillets
1/2 teaspoon capers
pinch chilli powder
125 g (4 oz) kalamata olives, pitted
3 tablespoons extra virgin olive oil
1/2 teaspoon chopped parsley
juice of 1 lemon
freshly ground black pepper

smoky chowder with cornbread

Janet Jeffs, Juniperberry

SERVES 4

60 g (2 oz) butter
3 bacon rashers, finely chopped
2 medium onions, finely chopped
3 celery stalks, finely chopped
60 g (2 oz) plain (all-purpose) flour
4 cups fish stock
440 g (14 oz) tomatoes, chopped
2 tablespoons tomato paste
a good pinch saffron threads
freshly ground black pepper
400 g (13 oz) smoked trevally or smoked cod
4 tablespoons cream

CORNBREAD
3/4 cup corn meal
1 1/4 cups plain (all-purpose) flour
1/2 cup sugar
1 1/2 teaspoons cream of tartar
1 teaspoon baking soda
1 teaspoon salt
1 egg, well beaten
1 cup milk
1 tablespoon melted butter

This is a perfect winter soup, best served with cornbread (sometimes called johnny cake).

First, make the cornbread. Preheat oven to 180°C (350°F). Sift together all the dry ingredients. Whisk egg with milk, then add butter. Combine the dry ingredients with the egg mixture, then pour the batter into a greased, shallow cake tin – about 23 × 13 cm (9 × 5 in) – and bake for 25 minutes.

While the corn bread is cooking, prepare the chowder. Melt butter in a large pan. Add bacon, onion and celery and cook for 10 minutes. Add flour, mixing well, then slowly stir in fish stock and simmer for 10 minutes. Add chopped tomatoes, tomato paste and saffron, and pepper to taste. Skin and bone the trevally or cod. Chop flesh into small pieces and add to chowder. Simmer gently for 2–3 minutes.

Ladle chowder into bowls, garnish with cream and serve with the warm cornbread.

Janet Jeffs was apprenticed to food legend Cheong Liew in Adelaide and has since worked with many of Australia's leading chefs in her 20-year career. She is executive chef and director of Juniperberry, and caterer to the National Gallery of Australia.

Juniperberry, National Gallery of Australia, Parkes, Australian Capital Territory 2600 (02 6240 6666); www.juniperberry.com.au

scarlet trout

Tim Pak Poy, Claude's, and Aaron Ross, The Wharf Restaurant

The idea of combining salmon (or ocean trout), beetroot and pinot noir began with master winemaker Max Lake in 1994. The following variation of this technique lends the fish sweetness, earthiness and vibrancy. After being marinated in beetroot juice, the ocean trout can be pan-fried, grilled, barbecued, or baked slowly as in the recipe below. A salad of finely cut grapes, roast walnuts, apple, celery and a little mayonnaise makes a good accompaniment.

Run enough peeled beetroot through a strong juicer to fill a deep, non-reactive dish large enough to hold the fish. Submerge the trout in the beetroot juice and add the crushed black pepper to fasten the colour. Store in the fridge for a minimum of 48 hours, turning the fish every 12 hours.

When ready to cook, remove the fish from the juice and place it on a rack set over a baking tray. Set aside until the fish has come to room temperature.

Preheat oven to 110°C (230°F). Season the fish generously with sea salt then place it in the oven on its rack with drip tray underneath. Cook gently to taste. We prefer it quite rare and suggest serving the trout at room temperature, sliced into 2 cm (³/₄ in) thick fingers.

Tim Pak Poy began cooking with Cheong Liew in Adelaide in 1983, then moved to Sydney to work with Anders Ousback and Damien Pignolet. He became chef and proprietor of Claude's in 1994 and has since won all of Australia's most prestigious food awards.

Aaron Ross supplied walnuts from his parents' farm to Tim Pak Poy, who eventually employed him in the kitchen at Claude's, where he excelled. Aaron is now head chef at The Wharf Restaurant.

Claude's, 10 Oxford Street, Woollahra, New South Wales 2025 (02 9331 2325); www.claudes.org

The Wharf Restaurant, Pier 4, Hickson Road, Sydney, New South Wales 2000 (02 9250 1761)

SERVES 6

raw beetroot for juicing – quantity depends
  on size of fish (see method)
1 side ocean trout, skin and
  pin bones removed
1 teaspoon freshly crushed black pepper
sea salt

celeriac, shallot and tomme de chèvre tart

Andrew McConnell, Diningroom 211

In this recipe, I'm trying to bind a group of compatible flavours with a custard – not dissimilar to a quiche (just don't ever call it that!). Tomme de chèvre is an aged goat's cheese, but fresh goat's cheese would also work.

First, make the pastry. In a food processor, pulse flour, butter and salt until the mixtures forms crumbs. While the processor is running, gradually add water until pastry dough forms. Do not overwork the pastry – as soon as it comes together, remove it from the machine. Cover and let rest in fridge for at least 2 hours.

Preheat oven to 180°C (350°F). Roll out the pastry to about 2 mm (⅛ in) thick and cut out one large, 20 cm (8 in) in diameter, or six small tart shells. Blind bake for about 12 minutes or until golden, then remove from oven and allow to cool, but don't refrigerate.

Meanwhile, prepare the filling. Sauté celeriac in olive oil until softened. Place shallots, sherry, sugar and salt in a small baking dish or tin, cover and roast for about 15 minutes. Roast hazelnuts on a baking tray for 3 minutes then rub them in a damp cloth to remove skins. Whisk together egg and egg yolks and fold in cream and thyme, adding salt, pepper and nutmeg to taste.

Fill the tart shell or shells with the sautéed celeriac and roast shallots, top with a little truffle paste (about 1 small teaspoon for each small tart or 1 tablespoon for a large tart, if using), tomme de chèvre and roasted hazelnuts, then pour the egg and cream mixture over the top so that the filling is barely covered. Bake the tarts for about 10 minutes until cooked and pale golden on top.

After training at some of Melbourne's best restaurants, **Andrew McConnell** relocated to 190 Queen's Gate in London, cooked on tour for Madonna and Prince, then headed east to Hong Kong's M on the Fringe. He and partner Pascale Gomes-McNabb now run Diningroom 211 in Melbourne.
Diningroom 211, 211 Brunswick Street, Fitzroy, Victoria 3065 (03 9419 7211); diningroom211.citysearch.com.au

MAKES 1 LARGE OR 6 SMALL TARTS

1 medium-sized celeriac, cut into
   1 cm (½ in) dice
2 tablespoons olive oil
10 golden shallots, peeled
2 tablespoons dry sherry
pinch sugar
pinch salt
1 egg
2 egg yolks
1 cup cream
1 teaspoon thyme leaves
salt, pepper and ground nutmeg
150 g (5 oz) tomme de chèvre
   or other goat's cheese
1–2 tablespoons truffle paste – optional
small handful of hazelnuts

PASTRY

500 g (1 lb) plain (all-purpose) flour
375 g (12 oz) cold, unsalted butter
1 teaspoon salt
125 ml (4 fl oz) sparkling mineral water

steamed pacific oysters with mirin and soy

Neil Perry, Rockpool

SERVES 4

½ cup mirin
3 tablespoons rice wine vinegar
3 tablespoons light soy sauce
1 small knob ginger, finely sliced
4 small red shallots, finely sliced
12 large, freshly shucked Pacific oysters
3 spring onions (scallions), finely sliced

This dish is best made with large Pacific oysters, such as those from South Australia and Tasmania. The sauce also works beautifully with steamed fish.

In a small saucepan, mix together mirin, vinegar, soy sauce, ginger and shallots and warm slightly. Set aside.

Put the oysters, in their half shell, into a steamer basket with the lid on and steam for 2 minutes to just heat through.

Arrange the oysters on a large plate and spoon a little of the sauce over each one. Sprinkle with the sliced spring onion and serve immediately.

Neil Perry is a leading ambassador for Australian food via his books, *Rockpool* and *Simply Asian*, and his television programs, but mostly through his cooking. His signature Rockpool restaurant has won many prestigious awards and in 2002 was named the fourth-best restaurant in the world by *Restaurant* magazine.

Rockpool, 107 George Street, The Rocks, Sydney, New South Wales 2000 (02 9252 1888); www.rockpool.com

confit of ocean trout with pea purée, braised fennel and a pernod and orange sauce

Peter Evans, Hugo's

This is one of my favourite dishes – it's silky, seductive, and very luxurious in the mouth. You can refrigerate the oil the fish was cooked in and dress a salad or some pasta with it.

Heat oven to lowest possible temperature – about 120°C (250°F). Put olive oil in a roasting tin large enough to hold the fish and place in oven to warm.

Place fennel in a saucepan with orange juice, Pernod, star anise and cinnamon stick. Bring to a simmer and cook the fennel until just tender. Reserve the cooking liquid for later.

Cut trout or salmon into six portions and bring to room temperature. Season with salt and pepper, carefully lower into the warmed olive oil and bake for 10 minutes, or until just medium-rare. Remove fish from oil to prevent it from cooking further.

While the fish is cooking, make the pea purée and the sauce. In a pan, bring 2 cups of water and a pinch of salt to the boil. Add peas, cook for 1 minute, strain, and refresh under cold water. Purée peas in a blender with 1 tablespoon of the butter. Season to taste. For the sauce, put the reserved fennel-cooking liquid in a pan and simmer until reduced by half, then add the other tablespoon of butter.

Heat a touch of olive oil in a frying pan, add diced pancetta or prosciutto and fry until crispy. Heat the pea purée and spoon a dollop onto each plate. Place the fish on the pea purée and spoon the sauce around it. Sprinkle the crispy pancetta or prosciutto into the sauce and stand the fennel out of the pea purée. Garnish with salmon caviar and a sprig of dill.

Peter Evans began his apprenticeship at The Pantry in Melbourne and liked it so much he bought into the business. He and his partners went on to open the award-winning Hugo's at Bondi Beach and Hugo's Lounge in King's Cross, and Peter plans to launch Hugo's Catering in Sydney in 2003.
Hugo's, 70 Campbell Parade, Bondi Beach, New South Wales 2026 (02 9300 0900)

SERVES 6

1½ cups olive oil
6 finger fennel, cleaned – or substitute baby
  fennel bulbs, cut into 2.5 cm (1 in) batons
3 cups orange juice
100 ml (3 fl oz) Pernod
1 star anise
1 cinnamon stick
625 g (1¼ lb) fillet of ocean trout
  or Atlantic salmon, in one piece
sea salt and freshly ground black pepper
500 g (1 lb) frozen peas
2 tablespoons butter
olive oil for frying
3 slices pancetta or prosciutto – optional
1 tablespoon salmon caviar
6 sprigs dill

chorizo-filled quail on spring onion flatbread with apple balsamic

Martin Beck, The Pantry

When sealing the quail, it's important to get it nice and golden brown so that the finished dish will be appealing.

Combine the chorizo, breadcrumbs, parsley, chopped garlic and chilli in a food processor and pulse into a paste. Transfer to a bowl and mix in the egg.

Preheat oven to 220°C (425°F). Use a cleaver to halve each quail, leaving the wing bone still attached to the breast. Place a spoonful of the chorizo paste between each wing and breast, then wrap each quail half in a slice of prosciutto. Lightly flour each quail parcel. Pan-fry the quail over moderate heat, for about 4–5 minutes each side, until golden brown. Remove from pan, place on a baking tray and cook in the oven for about 12 minutes.

To make the flatbread, place the flour, half the sea salt, pepper to taste, and the baking powder in a food processor. With the motor running, gradually add boiling water until a dough forms.

On a floured surface, roll out the dough, then brush with the combined vegetable, chilli and sesame oils. Sprinkle over the spring onions and the remaining salt, fold over and roll out again to spread the oil, spring onions and salt through the dough. Divide the dough into four balls. Flatten each dough ball to a thickness of 5 mm (¼ in). Pan-fry in a little olive oil until lightly browned on both sides – about 2–3 minutes on the first side and 1 minute on the other. Keep warm until ready to serve.

Combine balsamic vinegar and apple juice in a saucepan and reduce by half over high heat. Place the spinach, olive oil and sliced garlic in a hot pan or wok and cook until the spinach has wilted, stirring constantly. Stir through the lemon juice.

To serve, place a flatbread on each plate and top with some spinach. Place three quail halves on the spinach and drizzle apple balsamic around the plate.

Martin Beck trained under Guy Grossi at Caffe Grossi in Melbourne and worked with the Grossi family for most of his career. He has been at The Pantry restaurant, in the Melbourne seaside suburb of Brighton, since 2000.
The Pantry, 3 Church Street, Brighton, Victoria 3186 (03 9593 1533)

SERVES 4

2 chorizo sausages, roughly chopped
100 g (3 oz) fresh breadcrumbs
1 cup flat-leaf parsley leaves, chopped
1 teaspoon finely chopped garlic
1 teaspoon finely chopped fresh chilli
1 egg
6 quail – about 200 g (6 oz) each
12 slices prosciutto
plain (all-purpose) flour for dusting
¾ cup balsamic vinegar
1¼ cups apple juice
2 cups spinach leaves,
    washed and drained
2 teaspoons olive oil
1 garlic clove, sliced
juice of 1 lemon

FLATBREAD

4 cups plain (all-purpose) flour
6 teaspoons sea salt
freshly ground black pepper
4 teaspoons baking powder
2½ cups boiling water
4 tablespoons vegetable oil
1 tablespoon chilli oil
1 tablespoon sesame oil
4 spring onions (scallions), sliced
olive oil for frying

chilled cucumber soup with oysters

Scott Minervini, Lebrina

SERVES 4

1 large cucumber
1 spring onion (scallion), white part only,
   finely chopped
3 tablespoons lemon juice
¾ cup cream or thin yoghurt
salt and pepper
1 tablespoon finely chopped dill, or to taste
12 large oysters, live or very freshly shucked
lemon wedges

This soup is also great for cocktail parties, served in chilled shot glasses, with one oyster per glass. The combination of the brininess of the oysters and the cool smoothness of the soup is delicious.

Peel the cucumber and chop into large dice, then chop 1 tablespoon of the cucumber into small dice for the garnish and set aside.

Put the large cucumber dice, spring onion and lemon juice into a food processor and blend until smooth. Add the cream or yoghurt and season to taste with salt, pepper and dill. Transfer to a bowl and place in refrigerator until well chilled.

Shuck the oysters, if necessary, collecting any juices. Ladle the chilled soup into four small bowls (cups also work well) and place three oysters on top of each. Sprinkle with a little of the reserved oyster juices and the diced cucumber. Serve with lemon wedges.

Scott Minervini opened Lebrina restaurant in Hobart in 1994, using it to showcase Tasmanian food and wines and celebrate the delicate flavours of the island state.

Lebrina, 155 New Town Road, New Town, Tasmania 7008 (03 6228 7775)

Hobart, Tasmania

Sullivans Cove, Hobart, Tasmania

Friendly Beaches, Freycinet National Park, Tasmania

terrine of salmon gravlax and bluefin tuna

Alain Fabrègues, The Loose Box

Serve this easy terrine with a simple side salad of witlof (Belgian endive).

SERVES 6

500 g (1 lb) salmon gravlax, sliced
freshly ground black pepper
100 ml (3 fl oz) extra virgin olive oil
½ cup chopped dill
500 g (1 lb) sashimi-quality bluefin tuna
salt

Sprinkle water on a length of cling film twice the size of a 1.25 litre (2½ pint) terrine dish made of glass, stainless steel or clay. Squeeze out any excess water and line the terrine dish with the cling film, leaving enough overhang all around to cover the top of the terrine later.

Cover the edges and bottom of the terrine dish with gravlax slices, then season with pepper, olive oil and dill. Cut the tuna into slices 1 cm (½ in) thick and arrange in a layer over the gravlax. Season with salt, pepper, olive oil and dill. Continue to layer gravlax, tuna and seasonings until all the fish is used.

Fold the cling film over the top of the terrine and cover with a 1 kg (2 lb) weight – a small plank of wood, a clean brick or similar that fits over the terrine is ideal. Put the weighted terrine in the fridge and leave for 4 hours to set.

When ready to serve, use a sharp knife or an electric knife to cut the terrine into slices 1 cm (½ in) thick. Lay on a plate and drizzle with olive oil mixed with finely chopped dill.

The cooking of Frenchman **Alain Fabrègues** has been honoured in both his homeland and his adopted country. The Loose Box is a former Australian restaurant of the year, and Fabrègues has been declared Western Australian chef of the year five times.

The Loose Box, 6825 Great Eastern Highway, Mundaring, Western Australia 6073 (08 9295 1787); www.loosebox.com

asparagus and fontina tart with watercress and hazelnut salad

Russell Blaikie, Must Winebar

SERVES 6

1 brown onion, finely chopped
60 g (2 oz) butter
1 tablespoon picked thyme leaves
dash of white wine
sea salt and freshly ground black pepper
200 g (6 oz) fontina cheese, cut into
    1 cm (½ in) cubes.
3 small eggs
1 cup cream
12 medium-sized asparagus spears
extra virgin olive oil

PASTRY

250 g (8 oz) unsalted butter
350 g (11 oz) plain (all-purpose) flour
1 teaspoon salt
3 egg yolks
100–125 ml (3–4 fl oz) iced water

SALAD

2 tablespoons hazelnut oil
4 tablespoons extra virgin olive oil
1 tablespoon Bouquet de Muscat vinegar –
    you can substitute balsamic vinegar,
    but it is less sweet
2 teaspoons red wine vinegar
sea salt and freshly ground black pepper
250 g (8 oz) watercress, picked and washed
60 g (2 oz) hazelnuts, roasted
    and roughly crushed

Match this delicious tart with a glass of sauvignon blanc.

First, make the pastry. Cut butter into small cubes and chill in freezer for 10 minutes. If it is a hot day, chill the flour as well. Sieve flour and salt into the bowl of a food processor. Add butter and process for about 10 seconds – it should resemble coarse breadcrumbs. Add egg yolks and process briefly. With the motor running, add the water a little at a time until the dough holds together without being sticky. To test, squeeze a little between your fingers; if it crumbles, add a little more water. Do not process for more than 30 seconds. Roll the dough into a ball, wrap loosely in cling film and press flat. Refrigerate for at least 1 hour.

Preheat oven to 180°C (350°F). Roll out the pastry to a thickness of 5 mm (¼ in) and line a rectangular tart tin – about 36 × 13 × 2.5 cm (14 × 5 × 1 in) – with pastry, raising the edges approximately 8 mm (⅓ in) above the tin. Blind bake for 15 minutes, or until cooked through. Set aside to cool. Reduce oven temperature to 150°C (300°F).

Sweat onion in butter with thyme, white wine and plenty of salt and pepper until soft. Allow to cool. Line base of tart with onion mixture, and sprinkle the fontina cheese over. Whisk eggs and cream together, season well and pour into tart. Bake for 40–50 minutes, or until the centre is just set.

While the tart is cooking, make the salad. Whisk together hazelnut and olive oils and both types of vinegar to make a dressing. Season to taste, then toss with the watercress and sprinkle hazelnuts on top.

Peel the base of the asparagus, then cut each spear in half lengthwise. Cook for 2 minutes in boiling salted water, then season and drizzle with olive oil.

To serve, cut the tart into six, arrange four pieces of asparagus on top of each slice and serve with watercress and hazelnut salad alongside.

Russell Blaikie is a former Australian apprentice chef of the year who worked with Anton Mosimann at The Dorchester's Terrace Restaurant in London. He was a founding member of Perth's landmark Nº 44 King Street, and now cooks traditional Parisian and southern French bistro fare at Must Winebar, also in Perth.

Must Winebar, 519 Beaufort Street, Highgate, Western Australia 6003 (08 9328 8255)

tartare of tuna with goat's cheese
Tetsuya Wakuda, Tetsuya's

SERVES 4

250 g (8 oz) sashimi-quality tuna, finely diced
pinch ground white pepper
1 tablespoon olive oil
1 teaspoon finely chopped anchovies
60 g (2 oz) fresh goat's cheese,
    finely crumbled
3 teaspoons finely chopped chives
2 teaspoons soy sauce
2 teaspoons mirin
pinch sea salt
pinch cayenne pepper
¼ teaspoon finely chopped garlic
½ teaspoon finely chopped ginger
baby shiso and mâche (lamb's lettuce) leaves,
    to garnish

This dish works best when the goat's cheese used is not too salty.

In a bowl, mix together all the ingredients except the baby leaves.

Divide between four serving plates, and garnish with the shiso and mâche leaves.

Tetsuya Wakuda came to Australia from Japan in 1982 and opened the celebrated restaurant Tetsuya's seven years later. His unique skill in combining classic Western dishes with Japanese influences has earned him a reputation as one of Australia's finest chefs.

Tetsuya's, 529 Kent Street, Sydney, New South Wales 2000 (02 9267 2900)

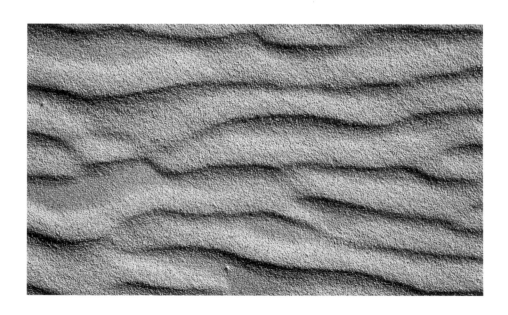

yabbies with celeriac remoulade

Damien Pignolet, Bistro Moncur

I think this is a marriage made in heaven – the sweetness of the shellfish meets the nuttiness of the celeriac. It is delicious with a good Australian sauvignon blanc.

Trim the leaves from the celeriac and peel it. Squeeze the juice of 1 lemon into a large bowl. Using a mandoline for preference, cut the celeriac into slices about 2–3 mm (⅛ in) thick. Using a sharp knife, cut these slices into even-sized batons and add to the bowl, tossing them well in the lemon juice.

For the remoulade mayonnaise, put the mustard, egg yolks, ¼ teaspoon salt and some pepper in a bowl and combine well. Gradually work in the olive oil with a wooden spoon to make a smooth, very thick emulsion. Taste for saltiness and adjust accordingly.

Strain the celeriac, but reserve the lemon juice. Mix the celeriac with sufficient mayonnaise to coat it, adding lemon juice and seasoning to taste. Cover and leave for 1 hour, to allow the flavours to develop.

Meanwhile, make a stock to poach the yabbies in. Combine the onion, celery, carrot, bay leaf, cracked peppercorns, thyme, lemon zest, wine, lemon juice and water in a large pan and bring to the boil. Allow to simmer for 20 minutes, then strain.

Slice the tops and bottoms off the grapefruit and run a knife against the flesh to remove the pith and skin. Working over a bowl, hold the skinned grapefruit in one hand and, with a small, sharp knife, cut on either side of the segments to release the flesh.

Return the stock to the pan and bring to a simmer. Poach the yabbies for about 2 minutes, then remove and allow to cool to room temperature. Shell the yabbie tails and crack the claws to make them easier to eat. Toss the tails in the extra virgin olive oil and some of the grapefruit juice, then add the grapefruit segments.

Using tongs, divide the celeriac between six plates, placing it to one side. Cut the witlof lengthwise into quarters and arrange in a pile beside the celeriac. Place the yabbie tails and grapefruit on top, decorate with a few claws, and serve.

Damien Pignolet is responsible for creating two Sydney eating institutions – Claude's, where he was executive chef and owner until 1993, then Bistro Moncur, where traditional French bistro fare takes on a uniquely Australian flavour.
Bistro Moncur, The Woollahra Hotel, 116 Queen Street, Woollahra, New South Wales 2025 (02 9363 2519)

SERVES 6

1–2 heads celeriac –
   about 500 g (1 lb) in total
1–2 lemons
1 heaped tablespoon Dijon mustard
2 egg yolks
salt and pepper
about 1¼ cups olive oil
1 small onion, sliced
1 stalk celery, sliced
½ small carrot, sliced
1 bay leaf
1 tablespoon cracked black peppercorns
a few sprigs of thyme
2 strips lemon zest
150 ml (5 fl oz) dry white wine
30 ml (1 fl oz) lemon juice or white vinegar,
   such as tarragon vinegar
6 cups water
3 pink grapefruit
18 yabbies or small freshwater crayfish
1–2 tablespoons extra virgin olive oil
3–4 small witlof (Belgian endive)

piri piri prawns
Steven Snow, Fins

Try to use prawns that have not been dipped in metabisulphate, a chemical solution used to keep them looking fresh. Ask your fishmonger for undipped ones – they have the sweetness and saltiness of real prawns.

Combine marinade ingredients well, then marinate prawns for 5–10 minutes.

Heat olive oil, garlic and chilli in a frying pan over high heat, then add prawns and coat well. Add Tabasco and season with sea salt. Turn the prawns, add chicken stock and cook for a minute or so, until prawns are just done.

Garnish with spring onions and serve.

Steven Snow studied business and law before deciding to become a chef. He lives and works in Byron Bay, on the north coast of New South Wales, where he grows many of the fresh herbs used at Fins – and only cooks nutritious, innovative food that he would want to eat himself.

Fins, Beach Hotel, Jonson Street, Byron Bay, New South Wales 2481 (02 6685 5029); www.fins.com.au

SERVES 4

16 large uncooked prawns (shrimp),
   peeled and deveined
1 tablespoon extra virgin olive oil
1 teaspoon chopped garlic
1 teaspoon chopped chilli
1 teaspoon Tabasco sauce
sea salt
½ cup rich chicken stock
2 tablespoons diagonally sliced
   spring onions (scallions)

MARINADE
½ cup lemon juice
½ cup extra virgin olive oil
1 teaspoon chopped chilli
1 teaspoon chopped garlic
2 teaspoons Tabasco sauce
½ teaspoon cayenne pepper

Cape Byron, New South Wales

roast quail breast with fat couscous, fried quail egg and yoghurt dressing

Guy Grossi, Grossi Florentino

SERVES 4

4 large quails – each about 200g (6 oz)
1 large carrot
1 stalk celery
1 large onion
salt and pepper
olive oil for frying
½ cup flat-leaf parsley leaves, chopped
2 tablespoons picked thyme leaves
1 clove garlic, finely chopped
200 g (6 oz) fat (coarse-grain) couscous
about 3 cups chicken stock
1 tablespoon butter
4 quail eggs
fresh herbs – chervil, coriander
   (cilantro), parsley, dill
a little olive oil, extra

MARINADE

½ cup flat-leaf parsley leaves, chopped
2 tablespoons picked thyme leaves
1 clove garlic, finely chopped
1 small red chilli, finely chopped
salt and pepper
200 ml (6 fl oz) olive oil

DRESSING

100 ml (3 fl oz) sheep's yoghurt
1 tablespoon verjuice
salt and pepper

This recipe combines the wonderful texture of quickly cooked quail breasts with the more intense flavours of the slowly cooked legs infused through the couscous.

Combine all the marinade ingredients in a large bowl. Place the quails on a board. Using a large knife or cleaver, separate the legs and thighs from the breasts, leaving the breasts on the carcass. Marinate the quail breasts for about 30 minutes.

Preheat the oven to 200°C (400°F). Chop half the carrot, celery and onion into rough chunks, reserving the other halves. Place the rough-cut vegetables in a shallow roasting tin and place the quail legs on top. Season with salt and pepper. Roast in the oven for about 10–15 minutes.

Meanwhile, chop the remaining vegetables into small dice and fry in a little olive oil, together with the parsley, thyme and garlic. Add the couscous and fry a little before adding some stock (don't add all the stock at once – you may not need it all). Cook the couscous, adding stock bit by bit, until it is fully cooked but still slightly al dente – about 15 minutes.

Remove the quail legs from the oven, and turn the oven down to 180°C (350°F). Take the meat from the quail legs and add it to the couscous. (The vegetables cooked with the quail legs can also be chopped and added to the couscous, if desired.) Add the butter, stirring it through the couscous as it melts.

For the dressing, put the yoghurt in a bowl with the verjuice, season with salt and pepper and mix together.

Briefly sear the marinated quail breasts in a hot pan with a little oil then put into the oven for 4 minutes. In another pan, fry the quail eggs in a little olive oil over a low heat until the whites are cooked but the yolks are still runny. Remove the quail breasts from the oven and separate the meat from the carcass.

To serve, put some of the couscous in the middle of each plate, place the quail breasts on top, then the fried quail egg. Drizzle the yoghurt dressing around, and garnish with the fresh herbs dressed with a little olive oil.

Guy Grossi has been cooking and promoting Italian food for more than 20 years – first at the restaurants his family founded, such as the respected Café Grossi, then at the restaurant his family bought, Grossi Florentino, a Melbourne culinary landmark. **Grossi Florentino**, 80 Bourke Street, Melbourne, Victoria 3000 (03 9662 1811); www.grossiflorentino.com.au

gyoza of pork and chinese cabbage with sautéed brussels sprouts

Karen White, Verge

SERVES 8 (MAKES ABOUT 32 GYOZA)

300 g (10 oz) lean pork mince (ground pork)
100 g (3½ oz) minced pork fat
¼ Chinese cabbage, finely sliced
1 tablespoon freshly grated ginger
½ cup chopped coriander (cilantro) leaves
50 g (2 oz) onion, finely chopped
50 g (2 oz) leek, finely chopped
50 g (2 oz) celery, finely chopped
salt and pepper
1 packet round gyoza wrappers
vegetable oil for frying
250 g (8 oz) brussels sprouts, finely sliced

DRESSING
150 ml (5 fl oz) mirin
60 ml (2 fl oz) sake
100 ml (3 fl oz) soy sauce
50 ml (1½ fl oz) red wine vinegar
1 tablespoon sliced ginger

These Chinese-style dumplings (also called pot-stickers) make a flavourful starter, or even a light meal with some steamed rice. Any extra gyoza can be frozen and cooked straight from the freezer – just give them a couple of minutes longer to cook.

Place all the dressing ingredients in a pan and warm slowly to allow the ginger to infuse the dressing, and to combine all the flavours. Set aside at room temperature.

Mix the pork, pork fat, cabbage, ginger, coriander, onion, leek and celery together. Make a 'tester' in the shape of a mini-burger and shallow-fry over medium heat in a little vegetable oil. Do not let it colour too much, as this will alter the taste. Test for flavour, and add salt and pepper until you are happy with the pork mixture.

Keep the gyoza wrappers in the packet, removing only one at a time to keep them from drying out. Put about 1 teaspoon of the pork mixture inside a wrapper and fold into a half-moon shape. Pleat the edges together, ensuring the gyoza are sealed properly.

Heat 1 tablespoon of vegetable oil in a heavy based frying pan over high heat and fry the gyoza in batches of about six. Brown the bottom of the gyoza, watching that they don't burn, then carefully add water to the pan until it's about two-thirds full – the oil may spit a little. Put a lid on the pan and cook the gyoza until the water has been absorbed (about 5–6 minutes). This method will steam the gyoza and give them a crispy-fried bottom. Keep the first batch of gyoza warm in a low oven while you cook the remaining gyoza in the same way.

In a separate pan, quickly fry the brussels sprouts in a little vegetable oil, ensuring they retain some crunch. Season to taste.

To serve, place sprouts on a plate, arrange gyoza on top and drizzle the dressing over them.

English-born **Karen White** worked in London and Paris (The Canteen, Hotel Nikko) before travelling around Australia and deciding to stay. She is head chef and co-owner at Verge, in Melbourne.
Verge, 1 Flinders Lane, Melbourne, Victoria 3000 (03 9639 9500)

cotechini, rabbit and fennel broth

Chris Taylor, Fraser's Restaurant

I really like the stickiness of cotechini sausage – it's fantastic with rabbit. This is a soup made for sharing: put a big bowl in the middle of the table and enjoy it with friends over a robust wooded chardonnay or a cabernet.

In a large, heavy-based saucepan, sweat the onion, fennel, celery, garlic, pumpkin and thyme with a little olive oil for 5 minutes.

Meanwhile, heat 2 tablespoons of olive oil in a frying pan until almost smoking. Brown the rabbit legs until well sealed, then add them to the onion and fennel mixture. Pour in 5 cups of the chicken stock and bring to the boil. Add the black-eyed beans, reduce heat to a simmer and cook for 30 minutes.

Pour the rest of the stock into another pan, add the whole cotechini and simmer for 15–20 minutes. Remove the cotechini, let it drain on kitchen paper, then skin and slice it and add it to the soup. Season to taste with salt and pepper.

When ready to serve, remove the meat from the pan and break the rabbit leg into bite-sized pieces. Pour the soup into four bowls, making sure there are more vegetables than liquid in each bowl, then divide the rabbit pieces and cotechini between the servings.

Shave some parmesan on top and drizzle over a little extra virgin olive oil.

Originally from country Victoria, **Chris Taylor** is now widely acknowledged as one of Western Australia's finest chefs. His Kings Park restaurant, Fraser's, has won many state and national awards since opening in 1993.

Fraser's Restaurant, Fraser Avenue, Kings Park, West Perth, Western Australia 6005 (08 9481 7100); www.frasersrestaurant.com.au

SERVES 4

¼ onion, diced
1 large fennel bulb, diced
2 small stalks celery, diced
3 cloves garlic, minced
250 g (8 oz) butternut pumpkin, diced
3 sprigs thyme
olive oil for frying
2 boned rabbit legs
8 cups chicken stock
125 g (4 oz) black-eyed beans,
    soaked overnight
about 500 g (1 lb) cotechini sausage
salt and cracked black pepper
parmesan
extra virgin olive oil

sea scallops with zucchini baba ghanouj and sauce jacqueline

Ian Curley

SERVES 4

8 large sea scallops
sea salt and freshly ground black pepper
1 tablespoon chopped chives
1–2 tablespoons fine strips of snow pea
    and pea shoots

ZUCCHINI BABA GHANOUJ

6 large zucchini (courgettes)
rock salt for roasting
1 tablespoon tahini
1 tablespoon lemon juice
100 ml (3 fl oz) yoghurt
sea salt and freshly ground black pepper

SESAME SEED TUILLES

5 egg whites
90 g (3 oz) flour
pinch salt
pinch black pepper
60 g (2 oz) butter, melted and cooled
1 teaspoon each of black and white
    sesame seeds

SAUCE

150 g (5 oz) butter
5 carrots, grated
12 cardamom pods
1 star anise
½ cinnamon stick
1 cm (½ in) ginger root, sliced
100 ml (3 fl oz) extra dry vermouth
2 cups fish stock
1 cup cream
sea salt and freshly ground black pepper
500 g (1 lb) frozen peas
¾ cup olive oil

The textures in this dish – the softness of the scallops and the crispiness of the sesame seed tuilles – go well together.

First make the baba ghanouj. Prick zucchini with a fork and roast on a bed of rock salt in a hot oven, 220°C (425°F), until soft to touch. Remove from oven and scoop out flesh. Hang zucchini flesh in muslin (cheesecloth) over a bowl for at least an hour – overnight is better – to remove excess liquid, then combine in another bowl with tahini, lemon juice and yoghurt. Season to taste.

To make the sesame seed tuilles, whisk egg whites until frothy but not yet forming stiff peaks, then fold in flour and seasoning. Fold in butter and rest for 30 minutes. Thinly spread onto non-stick baking paper then, using a skewer, outline the shape you want your tuilles (we do oblongs or star shapes) – you'll need to make eight to serve four people. Sprinkle sesame seeds over the top and bake in a 180°C (350°F) oven until golden brown – about 10 minutes.

For the sauce Jacqueline, heat butter in a large, heavy-based pan and add carrot, cardamom, star anise, cinnamon and ginger. Sweat ingredients for a few minutes to bring out the colour in the carrots. Add vermouth and simmer for 15 minutes. Add fish stock, bring to the boil and then simmer for 30 minutes. Strain the stock into a fresh pan and reduce over a high heat until 'sticky'. Add cream and reduce until it becomes pale mustard-orange in colour. Season to taste. Make pea oil by blending the peas with the olive oil, then straining.

Sear scallops in a hot frying pan for approximately 20–30 seconds on each side. Season, then combine with the snow pea and pea shoots.

To serve, place some baba ghanouj in the centre of each plate. Place one scallop on top of the baba ghanouj, then a sesame seed tuille, followed by another scallop and finishing with a tuille on top. Froth the sauce Jacqueline and the pea oil with a hand-held mixer, add the chopped chives, then drizzle over each plate.

Ian Curley was born in London, did his training there at The Savoy and the Hyatt, and made his name at several Melbourne restaurants – Rhubarbs, Stella, The Point and the Beaumaris Pavilion – since migrating in 1981.

salad of beetroot, asparagus, mâche and goat's cheese

Peter Doyle, est

Beetroot and goat's cheese are meant to go together – they're a classic combination.

Mix vinaigrette ingredients together, seasoning to taste with salt and pepper.

Boil beetroot for about 10–15 minutes until cooked. Remove from heat and allow to cool. Peel beetroot and, over a plate or bowl to capture the juices, cut into small wedges.

Cook asparagus in salted boiling water for about 3 minutes. Remove, drain well, season and toss with a little vinaigrette.

Toss beetroot with vinaigrette and arrange on plates, leaving a space in the centre. Toss mâche and curly endive in vinaigrette and place in centre of beetroot. Arrange the dressed asparagus on the salad and sprinkle toasted pine nuts on top.

Slice the goat's cheese and arrange on the salad. Sprinkle with chives and chervil sprigs. Mix a little of the beetroot cooking juices with an equal amount of vinaigrette and spoon around the salad. Serve immediately.

Peter Doyle is a surfer and a star of Sydney's restaurant scene. He and his partner, Beverley, established the landmark Le Trianon restaurant (later renamed Cicada) and Celsius. He is currently head chef at est.

est, The Establishment, Level 1, 252 George Street, Sydney, New South Wales 2000 (02 9240 3010)

SERVES 4

2 medium-sized beetroot
20 asparagus spears, peeled
sea salt and pepper
10–12 leaves mâche (lamb's lettuce)
½ small curly endive, pale inner leaves only
2 tablespoons pine nuts, toasted
200 g (6 oz) fresh goat's cheese
1 tablespoon chopped chives
8 sprigs chervil

VINAIGRETTE
60 ml (2 fl oz) walnut oil
60 ml (2 fl oz) olive oil
30 ml (1 fl oz) red wine vinegar
sea salt and pepper

mains

Cottesloe Beach, Western Australia

linguine with slow-roasted pumpkin, chilli, rocket and lemon

Sean Moran, Sean's Panaroma

The beauty of the chilli oil used in this recipe is that the oil left over can be kept for months and is handy to have in the pantry – use it as the base for Asian-style dressings or to add a little heat to pasta sauces.

Split chillies lengthways and remove seeds. Place in a heavy-based pan with oil and whole garlic cloves and gently cook over a moderate heat until all the moisture from the chilli and garlic has evaporated – the mixture should appear golden and smell nutty. Remove from heat and allow to cool. Strain, purée chilli and garlic to a smooth paste then stir back into the oil. Store in a sterilised glass jar.

Preheat oven to 150°C (300°F). On stovetop, heat enough olive oil in a heavy-based roasting tin to cover the bottom. Add pumpkin chunks and season with salt and pepper. When they are just starting to colour, turn the chunks and place roasting tin in oven until pumpkin is completely caramelised – about 1 hour. Place tin back on stovetop, add minced garlic and cumin, and toss gently until garlic is golden.

Bring a large pan of salted water to the boil and throw in linguine. While the pasta is cooking, combine all the other ingredients – pumpkin, about 2–3 tablespoons of the chilli oil, lemon juice, parmesan and rocket – in a large bowl. When the linguine is 'al dente', drain and toss with the rest of the ingredients. Season to taste and serve immediately.

Sean's Panaroma has become a Bondi Beach institution since opening in 1993. **Sean Moran**, head chef and owner, has worked with some of Australia's most talented chefs, including Gay Bilson, Anders Ousback, Neil Perry and Stefano Manfredi.

Sean's Panaroma, 270 Campbell Parade, Bondi Beach, New South Wales 2026 (02 9365 4924)

SERVES 4

125 g (4 oz) mild long red chillies
1 cup olive oil
2 cloves garlic, peeled
olive oil for frying
625 g (1¼ lb) pumpkin – ideally
   Queensland blue – peeled
   and cut into bite-size chunks
salt and pepper
1 clove garlic, minced
1 teaspoon ground cumin
500 g (1 lb) linguine
juice of 1 lemon
handful of roughly grated parmesan
handful of washed and shredded
   rocket (arugula)

gorgonzola gnocchi with garlic and sage butter, broad beans and crispy jamon

Daniel Myers, The Victoria Hotel

This is a really quick, fresh dish, and you can substitute peas or asparagus for the broad beans, depending on what's in season.

Boil the potatoes in their skins, drain, peel and mash in a food processor, or by hand. Add the flour, gorgonzola, and salt and pepper to taste. Combine well, then roll out into long logs about 2 cm (1 in) diameter. Cut into individual gnocchi about 1.5 cm (²⁄₃ in) thick. Bring a large pan of salted water to the boil, add the gnocchi and cook until they all rise to the surface. Drain.

Preheat oven to 180°C (350°F). Lay the slices of jamon or prosciutto flat on a drying rack, or on a baking tray lined with baking paper. Dry in the oven for 15 minutes, or until crispy.

Bring a pan of salted water to the boil and blanch the broad beans for 1 minute. Refresh under cold water and peel.

In a frying pan over low heat, soften the butter and add the garlic. Sauté until the garlic softens, then add the sage leaves. Sauté the gnocchi in the garlic and sage butter for 2 minutes, add the broad beans to warm through, then divide between four plates. Crumble the crisp jamon or prosciutto over the top, and serve.

Daniel Myers was so keen to get an apprenticeship that he accepted a job at a rough Victorian coastal pub popular with bikers. He soon fled to Melbourne, where he cooked with Michael Bacash at Toofey's and Philippe Mouchel at Langton's. He is currently head chef at the award-winning Victoria Hotel in Port Fairy, on the Great Ocean Road.

The Victoria Hotel, 42 Bank Street, Port Fairy, Victoria 3284 (03 5568 2891); www.vichotel.com

SERVES 4

1 kg (2 lb) potatoes, washed
375 g (12 oz) plain (all-purpose) flour
75 g (2½ oz) gorgonzola
salt and pepper
125 g (4 oz) jamon or prosciutto
125 g (4 oz) shelled broad (fava) beans
220 g (7 oz) butter
4 cloves garlic, finely sliced
7 sage leaves

steamed atlantic salmon fillet with spring onions and coriander

Cheong Liew, The Grange

SERVES 4

1 × 1 kg (2 lb) fillet of Atlantic salmon,
   skin left on, rib bones removed
salt and freshly ground black pepper
2 teaspoons shaohsing Chinese cooking wine
6 spring onions (scallions), finely shredded,
   white and green parts separated
2 cm (³/₄ in) knob ginger, finely shredded
3 tablespoons light chicken stock
1 tablespoon light soy sauce
1 teaspoon sugar
3 tablespoons peanut oil
fresh coriander (cilantro) leaves, to garnish

This fish recipe lends itself to the Chinese approach . . . the idea is not to have fish with rice, but to have rice with fish – an important aspect of Chinese dining etiquette.

Season salmon with salt, pepper and half the rice wine. Place salmon in a bamboo steamer and steam over a gentle heat for about 3 minutes – the meat should still be pink. Strain off the juices and place fish on a serving plate. Cover with the shredded white parts of the spring onions and the ginger.

In a small pan, bring stock to the boil. Remove from heat and add soy sauce, remaining rice wine and sugar, then pour this over the salmon. Heat peanut oil in another small pan until smoking, add the shredded green parts of the spring onions, then pour over the fish.

Garnish with fresh coriander and serve immediately.

Malaysian-born **Cheong Liew** was awarded the Order of Australia Medal in 1999 for his services to food and for 'developing and influencing the style of contemporary Australian cuisine'. He is consultant chef to The Grange restaurant at Hilton Adelaide.

The Grange, Hilton Adelaide, 233 Victoria Square, Adelaide, South Australia 5000 (08 8217 2000); www.hilton.com

tuna salad

Steve Ritchie, Watt modern dining

Briefly zap the limes in a microwave to get the most juice from them.

Lightly dust the tuna with the two sorts of pepper and the sumac. Flash-sear on a very hot chargrill with a little olive oil until medium rare (about 1 minute each side). Drain tuna on kitchen paper before placing in refrigerator to chill.

Combine fish sauce, garlic, spring onion, lemongrass, palm sugar, lime juice, lime leaf and chilli sauce in a blender to make the dressing. Strain.

Sear the scallops over high heat in a little olive oil and butter until translucent.

Remove tuna from refrigerator, slice thinly and place in a bowl with scallops, rocket, mango and avocado. Add dressing, toss gently to combine, then divide the salad between two bowls.

Steve Ritchie has worked his way around some of Australia's best resorts and hotels for 17 years. He has cooked at Lizard Island, Bedarra Island and Palazzo Versace. He has been chef de cuisine at Watt modern dining since 2001.

Watt modern dining, riverside, Brisbane Powerhouse, 119 Lamington Street, New Farm, Brisbane, Queensland 4005 (07 3358 5464); www.watt.net.au

SERVES 2

2 × 250 g (8 oz) fresh tuna steaks
30 g (1 oz) freshly ground Sichuan pepper
50 g (1½ oz) freshly ground black pepper
10 g (⅓ oz) sumac
olive oil for frying
2 teaspoons fish sauce
1 tablespoon minced garlic
8 spring onions, white part only, chopped
½ lemongrass stalk, trimmed and
    finely chopped
30 g (1 oz) palm sugar, grated
juice of 2 limes
1 kaffir lime leaf, finely sliced
2 teaspoons sweet chilli sauce
8 sea scallops
butter for frying
50 g (1½ oz) fresh rocket (arugula), washed
1 medium mango, peeled and sliced
    lengthwise
1 avocado, peeled and cut into small wedges

sand crab and glass noodle omelette with a broad bean and fennel salad

Steve Szabo, Vanitas at Palazzo Versace

You can have this omelette for brunch, lunch or dinner.

First make the dressing: whisk all ingredients together and adjust seasoning.

In a large bowl, cover the noodles with boiling water and allow to stand for about 5 minutes, then plunge into cold water and drain well. Using scissors, snip into 6 cm (2½ in) lengths. Whisk the eggs and seasoning well, then add crab meat, spring onion, parsley and noodles and stir until well combined.

Over medium heat, melt the clarified butter – ideally in a Japanese omelette pan 20 cm (8 in) square. You can also use a large, non-stick frying pan, but then you'll need to cut the edges off the cooked omelette to make it an even thickness. Tip out any excess butter. Ladle half the omelette mixture into the pan and spread out evenly using the back of a fork. When it is nearly cooked, tip the pan forwards and, using a spatula, start to roll the omelette. When rolled, tip it out onto some kitchen paper. Repeat the process with the other half of the omelette mixture.

For the salad, gently toss together the chives, fennel, parsley, broad beans and truffle oil dressing until well combined. Season to taste.

Slice each omelette into six rounds (three per person). Arrange these in the centre of a large, flat plate, and top with some of the dressed salad.

Welsh–Hungarian **Steve Szabo** has worked with some the world's best chefs – Bernard Gaume, Alain Senderens and Gary Houillibeck among them – at top London restaurants like the Chelsea Room and Ma Maison. Since arriving in Australia in 1988 he has cooked at a succession of fine restaurants, including Jimmy Watson's and Mietta's Queenscliff, and now Vanitas.

Vanitas at Palazzo Versace, 94 Seaworld Drive, Main Beach, Queensland 4217 (07 5509 8000); www.palazzoversace.com

SERVES 4

50 g (2 oz) glass noodles
  (bean thread vermicelli)
12 eggs
salt and freshly ground white pepper
300 g (10 oz) cooked sand crab meat, picked
4 tablespoons finely sliced spring onions,
  green part only
3 tablespoons finely sliced flat-leaf parsley
1 tablespoon clarified butter (ghee)

SALAD

3 tablespoons finely sliced chives
300 g (10 oz) fennel bulbs, finely shaved
3 tablespoons finely sliced flat-leaf parsley
200 g (7 oz) blanched and peeled young
  broad (fava) beans

TRUFFLE OIL DRESSING

1 golden shallot, finely chopped
1 teaspoon Dijon mustard
2 teaspoons sherry vinegar
2 teaspoons truffle oil
3 tablespoons extra virgin olive oil
1 tablespoon Fino sherry

aubergine mixed fish with provençale vegetables, pesto and aïoli

James Mussillon, Aubergine

SERVES 6

1 red capsicum (bell pepper)
6 slices eggplant (aubergine)
12 slices zucchini (courgette)
1 red onion, sliced into rounds
2 tablespoons caster (superfine) sugar
¼ cup white wine vinegar
¼ cup balsamic vinegar
olive oil for brushing and frying
6 × 125 g (4 oz) fillets of blue eye or sea bass
6 × 100 g (3 oz) fillets of snapper or halibut
6 large prawns (shrimp) – preferably
   Yamba prawns
salt and pepper
200 g (6 oz) baby spinach leaves
2 teaspoons butter

AIOLI
2 egg yolks
1 tablespoon white vinegar
juice of 1 lemon
1 clove garlic, chopped
1 teaspoon Dijon mustard
1 cup vegetable oil
salt and pepper

PESTO
30 g (1 oz) pine nuts
1½ cups basil leaves, tightly packed
1 clove garlic, peeled and chopped
60 g (2 oz) parmesan, grated
1 cup extra virgin olive oil

This dish was originally conceived at The Square in London. Use the freshest fish you can find – tuna and marlin work well. The richness of the vegetables marries perfectly with the fish.

Preheat oven to 180°C (350°F).

For the aïoli, blend egg yolks, vinegar, lemon juice, garlic and mustard in a food processor and drizzle in the oil with the motor running until the aïoli has a creamy consistency. Season and set aside.

For the pesto, roast pine nuts on a tray in the oven until lightly coloured. In a food processor, blend basil, pine nuts, garlic, parmesan and olive oil. Set aside.

Turn up oven to 200°C (400°F). Brush capsicum with olive oil and roast in oven for about 10 minutes. Remove and set aside to cool a little. Turn oven down to very low – 120°C (250°F).

Sauté eggplant and zucchini slices in a little olive oil over medium heat until both sides are golden-brown. Transfer to a baking tray and keep warm in oven. Sauté onion rounds over medium heat for 2 minutes, then add 1 tablespoon of the sugar and the white wine vinegar. Cook slowly until softened. Add these to the baking tray and keep warm.

When capsicum is cool enough to handle, remove skin and seeds and cut flesh into strips. Cook the strips in a heavy-based pan over a low heat with balsamic vinegar and the remaining tablespoon of sugar until softened. Keep warm.

Lightly brush the fish and prawns with olive oil, season, and chargrill or barbecue the fish for about 4 minutes each side and the prawns for about 2 minutes each side. Meanwhile, wilt spinach in a pan over a low heat with the butter.

To serve, place some spinach in the centre of each plate, top with onion rounds and a fillet of blue eye. Layer on a slice of eggplant, then the snapper, then two slices of zucchini, then a prawn. Finish with a dollop of aïoli and strips of red capsicum, then drizzle some pesto around the plate.

Canberra-based chef **James Mussillon** has worked with France's Joël Robuchon and Sydney's Guillaume Brahimi. His food has won him many fans and awards, and he now has his own restaurant, Aubergine.

Aubergine, 18 Barker Street, Griffith, Australian Capital Territory 2603 (02 6260 8666)

Port Fairy, Victoria

Port Willunga, South Australia

venison tagine with couscous and saffron yoghurt

Aaron Carr, Vasse Felix

SERVES 4

1 tablespoon black peppercorns

14 saffron strands

1 cinnamon stick

1 tablespoon mustard seeds

2 allspice berries

3 tablespoons vegetable oil

1 onion, finely chopped

4 cloves garlic, finely chopped

1 knob ginger, peeled and finely chopped

4 venison shanks

6 cups beef stock

300 g (10 oz) fresh dates, pitted and
  roughly chopped

salt

100 ml (3 fl oz) sheep's yoghurt

250 g (8 oz) couscous, cooked as per
  packet instructions

1 tablespoon parsley leaves

This is a great dish – we use Margaret River venison and slow-cook it to produce a hearty winter dish that goes well with a shiraz or a cabernet.

In a heavy-based skillet over high heat, dry-fry peppercorns, eight of the saffron strands, cinnamon, mustard seeds and allspice for about 1 minute until aromatic, then pound into a fine powder with a pestle and mortar.

In a heavy-based, deep-sided frying pan or a large saucepan, heat vegetable oil, then add onion, garlic, ginger and pounded spices. Cook over medium heat for 2 minutes. Add venison shanks and continue to cook for a further 2 minutes, turning the shanks regularly. Add beef stock, then cover and simmer for 15 minutes. Add dates and simmer for a further 30–40 minutes, or until the meat is falling off the bone. Season to taste with salt.

For the saffron yoghurt, infuse the remaining six saffron strands in a little warm water for 20 minutes, then add to the yoghurt and stir well.

To serve, place a mound of cooked couscous on each of four large plates, place a shank on the couscous and pour over some of the cooking liquid. Top with a dollop of saffron yoghurt and sprinkle with parsley leaves.

Aaron Carr trained in Perth and has been executive chef at the award-winning Vasse Felix winery in Western Australia's Margaret River region since 1995.

Vasse Felix, cnr Caves Road and Harmans Road South, Cowaramup, Western Australia 6284 (08 9756 5050); vassefelix.com.au

Cape Mentelle, Margaret River, Western Australia

charred dory with mung bean and lime paste

William Suen, The Chairman and Yip

The mung beans for this recipe are easy to get from Chinatown and most health food stores – just remember to soak them the night before.

To prepare the paste, blend the soaked and drained beans, almond slivers, garlic, olive oil and vinegar in a food processor – it should be quite a thick paste. In a heavy-based saucepan, gently simmer the paste over low heat for about 20–30 minutes, stirring often to blend the flavours and cook the beans through. Remove from the heat, stir in the lime juice and honey, then season to taste with salt and pepper.

Preheat oven to 200°C (400°F). Season the fish with salt and a drop of soy sauce, then sear on a hot barbecue or chargrill for about 2 minutes each side. Smear the paste on one side of the fish, transfer to a baking tray and finish cooking it in the oven for about 10 minutes.

Meanwhile, place a frying pan or wok over high heat and pour in a little olive oil. Add the cabbage and chives and stir-fry for 1½ minutes. Season to taste with a little soy sauce then pile onto serving plates and rest the fish on top.

William Suen has been head chef at the Chairman Group, at Madam Yip and now The Chairman and Yip, for 16 years. He began his training at the age of 15 in Macau, where he got his first taste of East-meets-West fusion cooking. He has also worked in Hong Kong and Bangkok, mastering traditional Cantonese, Sichuan and Thai techniques.

The Chairman and Yip, 108 Bunda Street, Canberra, Australian Capital Territory 2601 (02 6248 7109)

SERVES 4

4 × 250 g (8 oz) fillets of John Dory,
   ocean perch or other white fish
salt and Japanese soy sauce
olive oil for frying
625 g (1¼ lb) Chinese cabbage,
   roughly chopped
2 tablespoons chopped chives

PASTE
1 cup green mung beans, soaked overnight
10 roasted almonds, cut into slivers
2 cloves garlic, peeled and chopped
2 tablespoons olive oil
1 tablespoon Japanese rice wine vinegar
2 tablespoons lime juice
1 tablespoon honey
salt and pepper

basque-style seafood stew
Dustin Rodgers, Star of Greece Café

The base for this stew is best prepared a day in advance and refrigerated, to allow the flavours to develop.

Heat a large saucepan and add olive oil. When hot but not smoking add bacon, garlic and chilli and fry for a minute or so. Add onion and fry for 1–2 minutes, then add capsicums, turmeric, paprika and saffron, and continue to fry on high heat for 2–3 minutes, stirring occasionally. Add tomatoes and chicken stock, bring to the boil, then reduce heat and cook for a further 30 minutes. Add potatoes, season with salt and pepper, and simmer until potatoes are cooked — about 10 minutes. The stew base can be prepared ahead up to this point and refrigerated overnight.

Reheat the stew base and add all the fresh seafood. When mussels and vongole have opened, and the remaining seafood is cooked (about 10 minutes), divide the seafood between six hot bowls (7 mussels, 9 vongole, 3 prawns, 1 whiting fillet and ½ crab in each). Sprinkle with chopped parsley and serve with fresh baguettes.

Dustin Rodgers started cooking at Maggie Beer's Pheasant Farm, in the Barossa Valley. He honed his skills in the UK at the Michelin-starred Pied à Terre, Michael's Nook, Chez Nico and The Aubergine. He is now happily ensconced at the Star of Greece Café, in Port Willunga, South Australia.

Star of Greece Café, Esplanade, Port Willunga, South Australia 5173 (08 8557 7420)

SERVES 6

¼ cup olive oil
200 g (7 oz) smoked bacon, diced
3 cloves garlic, halved
2 chillies, chopped
1 onion, diced
1 red capsicum (bell pepper), diced
1 yellow capsicum (bell pepper), diced
1 green capsicum (bell pepper), diced
1 teaspoon ground turmeric
1 tablespoon smoked paprika
4 strands saffron
1 × 400 g (14 oz) tin crushed tomatoes
8 cups chicken stock
3 large potatoes, peeled and halved
salt and pepper
3 blue swimmer crabs, halved
42 mussels, debearded
54 vongole (baby clams)
18 large uncooked prawns (shrimp), peeled and deveined
6 × 150 g (5 oz) whiting fillets
chopped flat-leaf parsley and fresh baguettes, to serve

Port Willunga, South Australia

madras grilled fish

Selvam Kandasamy, Hanuman

This is a classic dish from Tamil Nadu in southern India. We use the Northern Territory's famous barramundi, which stands up well to the strong flavours of the spices.

Scale and clean the fish then pat dry, or have your fishmonger prepare it for you. Make three deep gashes in each side of the fish.

In a blender, make a paste from the ginger and garlic, adding water as required. Combine the ginger and garlic paste with the chilli, turmeric, lemon juice, vegetable oil and salt to make a fine paste without any lumps. Rub the entire fish with the paste, then cover and place in the refrigerator to marinate for at least 2 hours.

Heat a grill plate to medium and lightly spray with olive oil. Place the fish on the grill, seal both sides, then turn every 3 minutes until golden brown and cooked through. Garnish with coriander leaves and lemon wedges, plus onion, cucumber and tomato slices, if desired. Serve with some simple boiled basmati rice.

Selvam Kandasamy was born in Madras, India, and worked for the Sheraton Hotel there before coming to Australia in 2000. He is head chef at Hanuman in Darwin.

Hanuman, 28 Mitchell Street, Darwin, Northern Territory 0800 (08 8941 3500)

SERVES 2

1 × 750 g (1½ lb) whole barramundi
  or snapper
60 g (2 oz) ginger, chopped
10 cloves garlic, chopped
1 cup mild chilli powder
2 tablespoons ground turmeric
¾ cup lemon juice
1 cup vegetable oil
2½ tablespoons salt
olive oil spray
1 tablespoon coriander (cilantro) leaves
2 lemon wedges
sliced onion, cucumber and tomato,
  to garnish – optional
boiled basmati rice, to serve

pasta with artichoke and broad beans

Chris Ogden, La Baracca Trattoria, T'Gallant Winery

SERVES 4

juice of 3 lemons
4 globe artichokes
2 cups vegetable stock
10 flat-leaf parsley stalks
3 cloves garlic, halved
2 tablespoons olive oil
salt
1 kg (2 lb) broad beans
500 g (1 lb) penne rigate pasta
6 cloves garlic, finely chopped
½ cup finely chopped flat-leaf parsley
1–2 tablespoons shaved parmesan
1 tablespoon chopped chives

We have our own vegetable and herb gardens at the T'Gallant vineyard, so we pick our own artichokes in season. Make sure you cover them with plenty of lemon juice during preparation or they will oxidise and go black.

Squeeze the juice of 1 lemon into a bowl of water. Remove the stalks from the artichokes, then peel them and cut into quarters lengthways. Slice 2 cm (1 in) off the top of each artichoke and discard. Remove the tough outer leaves and clean around the base with a vegetable peeler. Cut each artichoke in half and remove the furry roughage near the heart. Rub the cut surfaces of the artichokes all over with lemon juice as you work. Finely slice each half and drop into the bowl of acidulated water while you finish preparing the artichokes.

Remove the artichoke pieces from the water and place in a saucepan with the vegetable stock, parsley stalks, halved garlic cloves, a drizzle of the olive oil and salt to taste. Bring to the boil and simmer for about 8–10 minutes or until tender. Remove the garlic and parsley and set aside the artichokes with their stock.

Shell the broad beans and blanch them in boiling water for 2–3 minutes. Refresh in iced water. Peel off the outer skins and set aside.

Cook the pasta until 'al dente', drain and set aside.

In a saucepan over low heat, sauté the finely chopped garlic with the chopped parsley in the rest of the olive oil for 1 minute. Add the pasta, the artichokes with their stock, and a pinch of salt. Toss until combined. When the pasta is steaming, add the broad beans, adjust seasoning and serve with shaved parmesan and chopped chives.

Chris Ogden trained and worked as a chef in England before heading to the Bahamas and, eventually, Australia, where he has cooked and taught in the Blue Mountains, west of Sydney, and in Cairns.

La Baracca Trattoria, T'Gallant Winery, 1385 Mornington–Flinders Road, Main Ridge, Victoria 3931 (03 5989 6565); www.tgallant.com.au

pork loin cutlet with chinese cabbage

Lorenzo Pagnan, Lorenzo's Diner

Remember to marinate the pork the day before, and start the cabbage just as you light your barbecue so it will be ready at the same time as the meat.

Mix together the finely chopped ginger, garlic, chillies and 2 tablespoons of the vegetable oil, pour over the cutlets and marinate overnight in the refrigerator.

To make the chilli jam, place all the ingredients except the coriander, sugar and fish sauce in a heavy-based saucepan with the vegetable oil, and cook until quite tender and slightly burnt. Reduce the heat, cover and simmer gently for 15 minutes. Add the remaining ingredients and cook over high heat for 5 minutes. Allow to cool, then blend to a smooth consistency with a hand-held mixer or a food processor. Store the chilli jam in a sterilised glass jar in the refrigerator – it will keep for at least 2 weeks.

For the cabbage, place the remaining 2 tablespoons of vegetable oil, the sliced ginger, chillies and sliced garlic in a large pan and fry until slightly tender. Add the tomato paste and continue to fry until the paste starts to caramelise slightly. Add the cabbage and mix well. Reduce the heat, place a lid on the pan and cook until the cabbage is soft (about 10 minutes). Remove the lid and, over high heat, add the rice vinegar, coriander and sugar and cook for 3 minutes.

Place the pork cutlets on a preheated barbecue or chargrill, season with salt and pepper, then cook to taste. Wrap each cutlet in foil and allow to rest in a warm spot for 5 minutes.

To serve, place a mound of cabbage in the centre of each plate and place the pork on top. Dollop a generous spoonful of chilli jam on top. (If you prefer, you can warm the chill jam slightly, but I like the contrast between hot and cold.)

Italian **Lorenzo Pagnan** worked with budding food stars Armando Percuoco, Oliver Shaul and Neil Perry in Sydney before decamping to the south coast of New South Wales. At all his restaurants, from Lorenzo's Café to Ristorante Due Mezze to the present Lorenzo's Diner, Pagnan only ever cooks food he likes to eat.
Lorenzo's Diner, 119 Keira Street, Wollongong, New South Wales 2500 (02 4229 5633)

SERVES 4

2 knobs ginger, finely chopped
2 cloves garlic, finely chopped
4 red chillies, finely chopped
4 tablespoons vegetable oil
4 pork loin cutlets – each about 200 g (6 oz)
2 tablespoons finely sliced ginger
2 dried long red chillies, chopped
4 cloves garlic, finely sliced
1 tablespoon tomato paste
1 Chinese cabbage, shredded into
   2 cm (1 in) slices
2 tablespoons rice vinegar
1 cup chopped coriander (cilantro)
   leaves and stalks
2 tablespoons caster (superfine) sugar
salt and pepper

CHILLI JAM
1 red capsicum (bell pepper),
   seeded and roughly chopped
1 red onion, roughly chopped
4 cloves garlic, chopped
4 red chillies, chopped
1 lemongrass stalk, finely chopped
1 kaffir lime leaf, finely chopped
2 tablespoons vegetable oil
1/2 cup chopped coriander (cilantro) leaves
30 g (1 oz) caster (superfine) sugar
30 ml (1 fl oz) fish sauce

roast rack of lamb with herb couscous, tomato, peas and garlic confit

Chris Matuhina, Magill Estate Restaurant

Although there are several elements in this dish, the actual effort and time required are quite manageable. Ask your butcher to remove the top flap of the lamb racks and to trim the bones to about 6 centimetres (2½ inches).

Preheat oven to 200°C (400°F).

Seal lamb racks with half the olive oil in a hot pan until lightly coloured. Place on a baking tray, season lightly and place in the oven on a middle shelf for 12–14 minutes for medium-rare, or to taste. Leave lamb in a warm place to rest for 10 minutes before cutting – this allows the juices to be reabsorbed into the meat, giving it more flavour.

Meanwhile, prepare the couscous and the sauce. Put couscous in a medium-sized bowl and pour over the boiling water. Stir and allow to stand for 10 minutes. Add chopped herbs and remaining olive oil and season to taste.

Heat vegetable oil in a large pan until warm. Add garlic cloves and poach over low heat until soft but still firm – about 10–15 minutes. Remove garlic with a slotted spoon and, when cool enough to handle, peel off the skin. Drop peas into a small pan of rapidly boiling water, blanch for about 30 seconds, then drain and plunge into iced water to set the colour and stop them overcooking. Cut tomatoes into quarters and scrape away the seeds. Reduce stock by half to give you a well-flavoured sauce base, then add tomatoes, garlic and peas and gently heat through.

To serve, heat couscous in a small pan or steamer, then divide between four bowls, placing the couscous in the centre and surrounding it with the sauce. Cut each lamb rack into four and arrange on top. Serve immediately, with a full-bodied red wine.

Adelaide-born **Chris Matuhina** has worked with Australian masters Alan Weiss, Anne Oliver and Tony Bilson, done promotional tours for Penfold's to Canada and London, and became executive chef at Magill Estate Restaurant in 1999.
Magill Estate Restaurant, 78 Penfold Road, Magill, South Australia 5072 (08 8301 5551); www.penfolds.com/VisitPenfolds/MagillEstateRestaurant.html

SERVES 4

4 lamb racks – each about 300–375 g
    (10–12 oz)
3 tablespoons olive oil
salt and ground white pepper
125 g (4 oz) couscous
¾ cup boiling water
1 tablespoon chopped fresh herbs – I use
    equal amounts of flat-leaf parsley, tarragon,
    chives and thyme
2 cups vegetable oil
½ cup medium-sized garlic cloves, unpeeled
1 cup shelled peas – about 1 kg (2 lb)
    unshelled
4 large ripe tomatoes, peeled
2 cups chicken, lamb or veal stock

seaweed and dashi-salted yellowfin tuna with wasabi and sour cream mash

Teage Ezard, ezard at adelphi

Make the preserved cucumber at least a day in advance, to give the flavours time to develop – it will keep for up to a week in the refrigerator.

To make the preserved cucumber, peel cucumber, cut in half lengthways and scoop out seeds. Place cucumber in a bowl and cover with salt. Refrigerate for 1 hour. Meanwhile, place peanut oil, ginger, chillies and peppercorns in a wok and cook over high heat until ingredients start to turn a golden colour. Take off the heat, add vinegar and sugar, then allow this preserving liquid to cool. Remove cucumbers from refrigerator and rinse thoroughly. Pat dry and place in a sterilised jar. Pour over the cooled preserving liquid and store overnight in refrigerator.

For the ginger juice, stir sugar into combined water and vinegar until it dissolves. Add ginger and allow to stand for 5 minutes.

For the mash, peel and quarter potatoes. Place in a large pan of boiling salted water, and cook over medium heat until soft. Drain well, return potatoes to the pan and mash. Add cream and crème fraiche and keep warm.

When ready to serve, drain preserving liquid from cucumber and cut each half lengthways into four thin slices. Add wasabi to the mash and mix well. Place a dollop of mash in the centre of each plate and drizzle with a little ginger juice.

Clean the tuna of any veins (dark reddish parts) and slice into 5 cm (2 in) thick steaks. Combine salt, bonito flakes, nori and dashi, lightly sprinkle onto each side of the tuna steaks and sear in a very hot, heavy-based frying pan – without any oil – for 15 seconds on each side. Lay tuna steak on top of mash, and place preserved cucumber on top.

Teage Ezard trained under the exacting Hermann Schneider, then made a name for himself and his 'Australian free style' cooking at Guernica in Fitzroy, Melbourne. He opened his own restaurant, ezard at adelphi, in 1999, and it is now one of Melbourne's – and Australia's – finest.

ezard at adelphi, 187 Flinders Lane, Melbourne, Victoria 3000 (03 9639 6811); www.ezard.com.au

SERVES 6

1 kg (2 lb) sashimi-quality yellowfin
 tuna loin, in one piece
1 tablespoon sea salt flakes
1 tablespoon bonito flakes
1 sheet nori, finely chopped
½ tablespoon dashi

PRESERVED CUCUMBER

1 large cucumber
3 teaspoons sea salt flakes
100 ml (3 fl oz) peanut oil
1 knob ginger, finely sliced
2 long red chillies, finely sliced
2 teaspoons Sichuan peppercorns
¼ cup rice wine vinegar
50 g (1½ oz) yellow rock sugar, ground

GINGER JUICE

3 tablespoons caster (superfine) sugar
3 tablespoons water
3 tablespoons rice wine vinegar
3 tablespoons finely grated ginger

MASH

4 medium-sized Desirée potatoes
2 tablespoons cream
1 tablespoon crème fraîche
1 teaspoon prepared wasabi

fillets of reef fish with saffron beurre blanc

David Pugh, Restaurant Two

SERVES 6

12 new potatoes
1–2 tablespoons vegetable oil
6 × 150 g (5 oz) fillets of reef fish,
    such as red emperor or snapper,
    all skin and bones removed
a little softened butter
75 g (2½ oz) fresh spinach
1 tablespoon butter

SAUCE
2 pinches saffron strands
3 golden shallots, sliced
3 cups white wine vinegar
6 black peppercorns
3 cups riesling or other unwooded
    white wine
250 g (8 oz) unsalted butter, softened

Richer-flavoured fish, such as red emperor, snapper or pearl perch, are best suited to this dish as the saffron may overpower more delicately flavoured fish. Suitable fish from colder waters include monkfish and turbot.

Preheat oven and a baking tray to 200°C (400°F).

Bring potatoes to the boil in salted water and cook until a fork can be removed cleanly (about 5–7 minutes). Drain and keep warm.

While potatoes are cooking, heat vegetable oil in a non-stick frying pan over a medium heat and seal fish fillets well on both sides. Remove hot baking tray from oven and lightly butter it. Transfer fish to baking tray and cook in oven for about 6 minutes – thicker fillets may need a little longer.

For the beurre blanc sauce, place saffron, shallots, white wine vinegar, peppercorns and white wine in a heavy-based saucepan and bring to the boil. Reduce by three-quarters, then strain sauce into a stainless steel bowl and slowly whisk in the softened unsalted butter.

Toss spinach and the tablespoon of butter in a hot pan until the spinach has wilted (about 60 seconds), then divide evenly between six plates. Rest fish on spinach and spoon sauce around sides of fillets. Place potatoes alongside and serve.

David Pugh is originally from New Zealand. He worked at the Connaught Hotel in London before arriving in Brisbane in 1983, where he has worked at a succession of top restaurants including Allegro and Two Small Rooms. He has been head chef at Restaurant Two since 1998.

Restaurant Two, 2 Edward Street, Brisbane, Queensland 4000 (07 3210 0600)

pan-fried baby calamari with farro

Lucio Galletto, Lucio's

If you can't get farro – a type of wheat, also called spelt – you can substitute the hard Sardinian pasta fregola, or even couscous.

Use a sharp knife to slice under the eyes of the calamari to separate the bodies from the tentacles. Remove the skin and insides from the bodies and discard. Place the bodies and tentacles in cold water to clean them thoroughly. Drain, pat dry with kitchen paper and set aside.

Bring a saucepan of salted water to the boil, sprinkle in the farro and stir gently. When the water comes back to the boil, reduce the heat so the water is just simmering and cook for 10 minutes. Remove from the stove but leave the farro in the water.

Place a large frying pan with the 2 tablespoons of olive oil over high heat. When hot, add the calamari, season with salt and pepper, and cook for 2 minutes each side. Remove the calamari from the pan and drain on kitchen paper.

To serve, spoon the farro out of the water into a bowl. Add the tomatoes, basil, two-thirds of the extra virgin olive oil, salt and pepper, and mix lightly. Spoon the farro onto four plates, place the calamari on top and drizzle with the remaining extra virgin olive oil.

Gentleman restaurateur **Lucio Galletto** came to Sydney from Italy in 1977, opening Lucio's in Balmain in 1981, before relocating to Paddington in 1983. In 20 years Lucio's has earned a reputation for modern Italian food, impeccable service and fine art.

Lucio's, 47 Windsor Street, Paddington, New South Wales 2021 (02 9380 5996); www.lucios.com.au

SERVES 4

20 baby calamari – about 8 cm (3 in) long
125 g (4 oz) farro (spelt)
2 tablespoons olive oil
salt and pepper
2 vine-ripened tomatoes, seeded and diced
4 fresh basil leaves, torn
100 ml (3 fl oz) extra virgin olive oil

singapore chilli bean noodle with barbeque pork and apple salad

Lee Martin, Nº 44 King Street

SERVES 6–8

1 kg (2 lb) pork belly

peanut oil for frying

2 tablespoons unsalted peanuts

pinch dried chilli flakes

sea salt

1 kg (2 lb) fresh Hokkien noodles

¼ Chinese cabbage, shredded

1 medium-sized red capsicum (bell pepper), deseeded and cut into batons

1 medium-sized red onion, sliced

100 g (3½ oz) bean sprouts

6 spring onions (scallions), diagonally sliced

100 g (3½ oz) snow peas (mange tout), topped, tailed and halved

100 g (3½ oz) uncooked prawns (shrimp), peeled and deveined

MARINADE

4 tablespoons salted black beans, rinsed and drained

4 tablespoons shaohsing Chinese cooking wine

8 cloves garlic, finely grated

4 tablespoons hoi sin sauce

4 tablespoons dark soy sauce

1 teaspoon dried chilli flakes

2 cm (1 in) knob ginger, finely grated

2 tablespoons caster (superfine) sugar

4 tablespoons water

GARNISH

1 medium daikon (mooli), finely julienned

2 apples, finely julienned

1 long red chilli, seeded and very finely sliced at an angle

15 sprigs each mint and coriander (cilantro)

For a leaner version of this dish, you can use pork fillet instead of pork belly. The daikon, apple and chilli garnish should be very finely cut to look sharp and crispy – a contrast to the soft coriander and mint leaves.

In a bowl, whisk together all the marinade ingredients. Place pork belly in a shallow dish, cover with half the marinade and allow to marinate in refrigerator for 2 hours.

Preheat oven to 160°C (325°F). Remove pork from marinade and heat a little peanut oil in a heatproof casserole. Brown the pork, then pour the marinade back over it. Add 1 cup of water and cover with a lid or foil. Braise in oven until tender – about 1½–2 hours. Set aside to cool, then remove any excess fat, and slice pork thinly.

Over a medium heat, brown peanuts in a frying pan with a little peanut oil. Remove from heat and mix with the pinch of chilli flakes. When cool, roughly chop peanuts and season with a little sea salt. Set aside.

Bring a pan of lightly salted water to the boil and blanch the noodles for 30 seconds. Drain and set aside in a warm place.

Combine all the vegetables. In a wok, heat a little peanut oil and stir-fry vegetables, pork and prawns for 2 minutes. Add the remaining half of the marinade and cook for 1 minute. Add noodles, mix well, and immediately divide between six or eight noodle bowls.

Using your hands, toss the daikon, apple, mint and coriander, place a little on top of each bowl and sprinkle with some of the peanut and chilli mixture.

Lee Martin quit London for Australia and took up residence at the Lizard Island Resort in Queensland, where he was head chef. He has since worked his way around Australia and has been head chef at Perth's Nº 44 King Street since 2002. **Nº 44 King Street**, 44 King Street, Perth, Western Australia 6000 (08 9321 4476)

turkey saltimbocca

Stephanie Alexander, Richmond Hill Cafe and Larder

This variation on a much-loved classic is an excellent and unusual way to enjoy turkey. Turkey breast fillets are available from some supermarkets or you can order them from your butcher. The ones I buy are from small, free-range birds.

Reserve the small underfillet from the turkey breast for another dish. Slice the turkey breast fillet on the diagonal to yield twelve slices, each about 5 mm (¼ in) thick. One at a time, place each turkey slice inside a plastic bag and flatten using the flat side of a meat mallet. Lay a slice of prosciutto along each slice, press on two sage leaves, season lightly with freshly ground pepper and set aside, covered. Do not overlap the slices, as they may stick together.

Cut each fennel bulb into four thick slices, leaving them still attached at the base. Blanch in plenty of lightly salted boiling water until just tender. Drain thoroughly and pat dry. Heat olive oil in a frying pan and sauté the fennel slices for 5 minutes on each side, until golden brown. Transfer to a baking dish.

The cooking and saucing of the saltimbocca takes less than 10 minutes, so everything must be ready before you start. Preheat oven to 180°C (350°F), warm six dinner plates and have a pan of lightly salted boiling water ready for the peas. You will need two non-stick frying pans of 25 cm (10 in) diameter.

Place fennel in oven to warm. Lightly dust each turkey slice with plain flour. Divide clarified butter between the two frying pans and heat. Quickly add the slices of turkey, prosciutto-side down, and allow to sizzle over a brisk heat for 3 minutes. Meanwhile, drop peas into the pan of boiling water. Turn turkey slices – the first side should be golden, with the prosciutto slightly crisped. Cook for a further 3 minutes. Combine marsala and wine, turn the heat to high and divide the liquid between the two pans. Shake gently for a minute, then reduce the heat. Quickly transfer turkey slices to a hot plate to rest while you add butter and lemon juice to the pans. Shake and swirl to combine. Taste for salt.

Place two turkey saltimbocca on each plate with two slices of fennel and a spoonful of the drained peas. Spoon over the sauce.

Stephanie Alexander ran the acclaimed Stephanie's restaurant in Melbourne for 21 years. She is arguably Australia's best-known cook and food author; her seminal *The Cook's Companion*, published in 1996, has been praised as the most important food book published in Australia.

Richmond Hill Cafe and Larder, 48–50 Bridge Road, Richmond, Victoria 3121 (03 9421 2808); www.rhcl.com.au

SERVES 6

1 turkey breast fillet – about 1.2 kg (2 lb 6 oz)
12 thin slices prosciutto
24 sage leaves
salt and pepper
3 bulbs fennel
2 tablespoons olive oil
plain (all-purpose) flour for coating meat
²/₃ cup clarified butter
2 cups shelled peas –
   about 1 kg (2 lb) unshelled
100 ml (3 fl oz) dry marsala
100 ml (3 fl oz) dry white wine
60 g (2 oz) cold unsalted butter,
   cut into cubes
generous squeeze of lemon juice

linguette ai fiori

Tony Percuoco, Ristorante Fellini

This dish was created specifically for the celebration of summer, its rich colours representing freshness and vitality in food. Don't be shy with the salt – you need to coax out the natural flavours.

Add the pasta to a large pan of boiling, salted water and cook until 'al dente'.

Meanwhile, place a large, heavy-based pan on the stove over high heat. Add half the oil and, when hot, add the prawns, calamari and some salt and cook for a few minutes. Add the garlic, sliced zucchini and tomato, and a little more salt, and cook for 2 minutes. Add the wine and cook for a further 3 minutes.

Drain the pasta but do not rinse it – the natural starch helps the sauce to cling. Add the cooked pasta to the pan, stirring frequently, and sprinkle in the parsley and zucchini flowers, and the rest of the oil. Toss through well. Serve immediately, drizzled with a little more oil.

Tony Percuoco is a fourth-generation restaurateur who began his career at the Sydney Opera House in 1973. Fresh from his family's Sydney restaurant, Pulcinella, he opened Senso Unico, also in Sydney, before moving to the Gold Coast, where he opened the award-winning Grissini, and now Ristorante Fellini.

Ristorante Fellini, Waterfront Marina Mirage, 74 Seaworld Drive, Main Beach, Queensland 4217 (07 5531 0300); www.fellini.com.au

SERVES 4

400 g (13 oz) dried linguette, fettuccine or
  any long, flat pasta made without eggs
1/3 cup extra virgin olive oil, plus a little extra
250 g (8 oz) uncooked prawns (shrimp),
  peeled and deveined
200 g (6 oz) cleaned calamari,
  cut into rings or strips
sea salt and pepper
3 cloves garlic, finely chopped
100 g (3 oz) small zucchini (courgettes), sliced
3 roma (plum) tomatoes, peeled,
  deseeded and sliced
3/4 cup dry white wine
4 stems flat-leaf parsley, leaves picked
  and roughly chopped
12 zucchini (courgette) flowers, roughly torn

Gold Coast, Queensland

two-way tuna

Tippy Heng, Dish Restaurant and Raw Bar

This dish follows the Chinese principle of Yin and Yang, with the hot and the cold dishes balancing each other. The hot, pepper-crusted tuna should be consumed first – the heat of the pepper and the strongly flavoured sauce are the Yang elements – followed by the cold sashimi tuna salad with its subtle dressing.

For the sashimi, place walnut oil, sugar, rice wine vinegar, carrot, spring onion, radish and sesame seeds in a bowl and whisk together to make a dressing, adding salt and pepper to taste. Slice tuna into thin slivers and marinate in the dressing for 2 minutes. Toss well and arrange the sashimi salad on one half of each of four plates.

For the pepper-crusted tuna, coat tuna in pepper and coriander. Put 1 tablespoon of the peanut oil in a heavy-based frying pan over high heat and lightly sear tuna for 20 seconds each side, then set aside.

In a wok, heat the other tablespoon of peanut oil and the sesame oil, then fry the ginger and garlic until light golden in colour. Add soy sauce, Chinese cooking wine, sugar and, lastly, the bok choy leaves. As soon as the leaves have wilted, remove wok from heat.

To serve, slice the pepper-crusted tuna into four slices about 5 mm (¼ in) thick. Place the bok choy on the other half of each plate – opposite the sashimi – with a slice of tuna on top, and garnish with coriander leaves.

Tippy Heng was born in Laos, raised in Thailand, and moved to Australia in 1980, aged 7. He worked with Neil Perry at Rockpool for 4 years before heading to Byron Bay to become head chef at Rae's on Watego's. He has been chef at Dish since 1998.

Dish, Shop 4, Jonson Street (cnr Marvel Street), Byron Bay, New South Wales 2481 (02 6685 7320)

SERVES 4

SASHIMI

100 ml (3 fl oz) walnut oil
2 teaspoons caster (superfine) sugar
2 teaspoons Chinese rice wine vinegar
1 medium carrot, peeled and
   cut into thin strips
2 spring onions (scallions), thinly sliced
2 medium-sized white radishes
   (daikon), shredded
2 teaspoons toasted sesame seeds
salt and pepper
375 g (12 oz) yellowfin tuna
coriander (cilantro) leaves, to garnish

PEPPER-CRUSTED TUNA

375 g (12 oz) yellowfin tuna, in one piece
1 tablespoon freshly ground black
   peppercorns
1 tablespoon chopped coriander
   (cilantro) leaves
2 tablespoons peanut oil
2 teaspoons sesame oil
1 teaspoon crushed ginger
1 teaspoon crushed garlic
1 tablespoon light soy sauce
4 tablespoons shaohsing Chinese
   cooking wine
2 teaspoons caster (superfine) sugar
6 bok choy leaves

crunchy parmesan chicken

Kate Lamont, Lamont's East Perth

SERVES 6

9 tomatoes, cut in half
olive oil for drizzling
sea salt and freshly ground black pepper
3 stalks rosemary, leaves picked
4 stalks thyme, leaves picked
2 cups fresh breadcrumbs
1/2 cup chopped parsley
1/2 cup grated parmesan
12 chicken pieces *or* 1 large chicken cut
   into 12 – about 1.5 kg (3 lb) in total
125 g (4 oz) melted butter

SALAD

3 tablespoons chardonnay vinegar
2/3 cup robust olive oil
sea salt and freshly ground black pepper
assorted lettuce leaves
24 asparagus spears, blanched
3 avocados, halved and sliced

This is delicious served cold or at room temperature, and is lovely for picnics. A mix of chicken thighs and breast on the bone works best.

Preheat oven to 120°C (250°F). Place tomato halves, cut-side up, on a baking tray, drizzle with olive oil and sprinkle with salt, pepper, rosemary and thyme. Bake for about 1 hour, or until tomatoes have shrunk by half. Remove and set aside then increase oven temperature to 180°C (350°F).

In a bowl, mix together breadcrumbs, parsley and parmesan, and season with salt and pepper. Dip chicken pieces in melted butter then roll in the crumb mixture. Place crumbed chicken in a baking dish and bake for about 40–45 minutes.

For the salad, make a dressing by combining chardonnay vinegar with olive oil and seasoning with salt and pepper. Toss salad leaves in the dressing.

To serve, place some salad leaves on each of six plates and arrange two roasted tomato halves, four asparagus spears and some sliced avocado on the leaves. Top with more salad leaves, another tomato half and some more avocado. Rest two chicken pieces on top of the salad.

Kate Lamont's 15-year cooking career has focused on simple, delicious food to accompany wine. She is involved with her family's wineries in the Swan Valley and Margaret River regions of Western Australia, and has her own restaurant in Perth.

Lamont's East Perth, 11 Brown Street, East Perth, Western Australia 6004 (08 9202 1566); www.lamonts.com

Cottesloe, Western Australia

roast duck in a crust of fresh herbs and salt with sweet turnips and tasmanian beer

Meyjitte Boughenout, Franklin Manor

This is a perfect dinner after a brisk day on the windswept coast around Strahan. Get the skin of the duck nice and crispy over a high heat but be careful not to overcook it. The breast and legs are served separately here, over two courses.

Combine flour, salt, egg whites and all the herbs in a medium-sized bowl and mix until dough holds together. Knead for about 2 minutes until the dough is smooth and elastic. Wrap in cling film and leave in the fridge for about 30 minutes.

Preheat oven to 300°C (570°F), or as high as it will go. Prick duck skin all over with a fork, and season the duck inside and out with salt and pepper. Heat oil in a large, ovenproof skillet, add duck and brown on all sides for about 10 minutes. Transfer duck – reserving the juices in the skillet – to a roasting tin and place in oven for 10 minutes to sear it. Remove and set aside to cool, then turn down the oven to 180°C (350°F).

Turn dough out onto a lightly floured surface and roll into a rectangle large enough to enclose the duck. Place cooled duck in the middle, breast-side down. Wrap dough around duck, pinching to seal. Cook duck, seam-side down, in the oven for about 30 minutes.

Add turnips to the skillet containing the reserved duck juices and slowly caramelise them over medium heat until just tender. Deglaze the pan juices with vinegar and beer for about 5 minutes, simmering until the liquid is reduced by three-quarters. Add honey and veal stock, cook for 5 more minutes, then season to taste.

Remove duck from oven and use a sharp knife to cut through the dough crust. Peel it away from the duck and discard. Thinly slice the breast meat and arrange on plates. Spoon sauce and turnips all around, and serve as the first course.

Put the duck legs back in the oven until the skin crisps – about 15–20 minutes – then serve them, cut in half, as a second course. Accompany with a green salad.

French-born **Meyjitte Boughenout** worked under food legends Pierre Gagnaire and George Blanc, as well as other well-known chefs. After several years working in Sydney restaurants – at Merrony's and Claudine's – he moved to Singapore, before settling on Tasmania's West Coast, where he is now co-owner of Franklin Manor.
Franklin Manor, The Esplanade, Strahan, Tasmania 7468 (03 6471 7311); www.franklinmanor.com.au

SERVES 4

3 cups plain (all-purpose) flour
1/2 cup rock salt
10 egg whites
2 tablespoons finely chopped rosemary
2 tablespoons finely chopped thyme
1/2 cup finely chopped coriander (cilantro) leaves
1 whole duck – about 1.5 kg (3 lb)
salt and pepper
4 tablespoons olive oil
12 baby turnips, trimmed and peeled
2 tablespoons white wine vinegar
1 cup lager-style beer – ideally Tasmanian
2 tablespoons honey – ideally leatherwood
1/2 cup veal stock
green salad, to serve

whole baby barramundi with chinese black bean sauce and crisp noodles

George Francisco, Dish

Use a stockpot to fry the fish and put in two at a time, curving the fish against the sides. This way, your fish will be able to stand up on the plate and will look spectacular. Note that Chinese chilli paste with garlic is readily available from Asian supermarkets.

To make the black bean sauce, combine all ingredients except spring onions, tomato and butter in a pan over medium heat and bring to the boil. Add the spring onions and tomato, then turn off the heat and whisk in the butter.

Using a sharp knife, score the fish four times, running parallel to the gills. Mix together the flour, cornflour, salt and pepper and dredge each fish until lightly coated. Pour the oil into a large stockpot and place over medium–high heat. When the oil is hot but not smoking, carefully lower two fish into the oil, curving them around the sides of the pot. Fry for 5 minutes, or until the skin is crisp and browned. Remove and drain on kitchen paper. Repeat the process with the remaining fish, being sure to allow the oil to heat up again between each batch. After removing the last batch of fish, skim the oil, then reheat, ready for the noodles.

Carefully drop the noodles in the oil and cook for 30 seconds, or until they are crisp and light. Remove and drain on kitchen paper.

To serve, ladle some of the black bean sauce onto each plate, set the fish on top and place some noodles on the side. Garnish with coriander as desired.

US-born **George Francisco** was trained in San Francisco by Jeremiah Tower (Stars Restaurant) before becoming head chef at the respected Farallon. He came to Australia in 2002 and is owner and executive chef at Dish, on Sydney's northern beaches.

Dish Café Restaurant, 352 Barrenjoey Road, Newport, New South Wales 2106 (02 9999 2398)

SERVES 6

6 × 500 g (1 lb) whole baby barramundi
    or sea bass, scaled and gutted
1 cup plain (all-purpose) flour
1 cup cornflour (cornstarch)
salt and pepper
8 cups vegetable oil
6 cups fresh thin egg noodles *or*
    250 g (8 oz) dried thin egg noodles
fresh coriander (cilantro) sprigs, to garnish

BLACK BEAN SAUCE
1 cup Chinese fermented black beans,
    rinsed thoroughly
¼ cup honey
6 tablespoons sesame oil
2 tablespoons Chinese chilli paste with garlic
¼ cup rice vinegar
6 tablespoons fish sauce
¼ cup soy sauce
3 tablespoons finely chopped pickled ginger
1 tablespoon finely chopped fresh ginger
1 clove garlic, finely diced
6 tablespoons chopped coriander
    (cilantro) leaves
6 tablespoons finely sliced
    spring onions (scallions)
½ cup seeded and diced tomato
25 g (1 oz) butter

fillet of pepper-glazed beef with oven-roasted carrot and parsnip, topped with saffron chèvre

Donna O'Sullivan, The Blue Fig

SERVES 4

12 baby carrots
1 large parsnip
2 tablespoons unsalted butter
4 tablespoons honey
salt and pepper
4 cups strong beef stock
½ cup sugar
3 tablespoons water
¾ cup red wine
2 tablespoons coarse-milled pepper
1 tablespoon olive oil
1 teaspoon ground turmeric
¼ cup white wine
8 saffron strands
125 g (4 oz) goat's cheese (chèvre)
olive oil for frying
4 pieces fillet steak – each 250 g (8 oz)
splash of red wine, extra
8 chives

Make sure you reduce the pepper glaze right down, otherwise it won't coat the beef properly or give the sauce a glossy finish.

Preheat oven to 180°C (350°F).

Trim carrots to leave 1 cm (½ in) of the green tips. Cut parsnip into batons the same size as the carrots, discarding the central core. Place vegetables on a baking tray, dot with butter, drizzle with honey and season with salt and pepper. Bake for 10–15 minutes, until golden. Remove from oven and cover with foil to keep warm.

Place stock in saucepan and reduce over medium heat until you're left with about 1 cup of concentrated stock.

Make a pepper glaze by placing sugar and water in a saucepan to caramelise over medium–high heat for 3–5 minutes. Once sugar has turned golden, add red wine and pepper. Cook for about 10 minutes until the glaze has a thick, syrupy consistency.

Heat the tablespoon of olive oil in a small saucepan, add turmeric, white wine and saffron. Bring to the boil then remove from stove and allow to cool. Slice the goat's cheese into four discs, lay on a plate and cover with the cooled saffron liquid.

Preheat oven to 200°C (400°F). Heat a little olive oil in a large frying pan over high heat and seal the fillet steaks, then spoon over half the pepper glaze. Remove beef to a baking tray and place a disc of goat's cheese on each fillet. Finish in the oven to desired degree – about 4 minutes for rare, 8 minutes for medium-rare, 12 minutes for well done. At the same time, return carrot and parsnip to the oven to heat through.

Deglaze the beef pan with the extra splash of red wine, then add the reduced stock and the remaining pepper glaze. Simmer the sauce until it is shiny and slightly thickened.

Put carrot and parsnip in the centre of each of four warm plates. Remove beef from oven and place fillets on top of the vegetables. Spoon the sauce on either side of the beef. Garnish the chèvre with chives, then serve.

Donna O'Sullivan learnt her craft at Ziggy's, then at Pegrum's under Mark Armstrong. She took over the kitchen at The Blue Fig, on the mid-north coast of New South Wales, in 2002.
The Blue Fig, 23 First Avenue, Sawtell, New South Wales 2452 (02 6658 4334)

Fishing Boat Harbour, Fremantle, Western Australia

Byron Bay Hinterland, New South Wales

lamb ragout with maltagliatti pasta

David Matthews, Augé

Do all your preparation – including cooking the lamb racks – beforehand, so you can spend more time with your guests. Make the ragout the day before, to allow time for the flavours to develop.

Dry-fry fennel seeds in a heavy-based pan until aromatic, then grind in a mortar and pestle. Sauté celery, onion, carrot, garlic and ground fennel in 1 tablespoon of olive oil until tender. Add diced lamb shoulder and chicken stock and bring to a gentle simmer. Simmer for 2 hours or until meat is tender. If preparing the ragout a day ahead, allow to cool before refrigerating overnight.

To make the pasta, mix eggs and breadcrumbs well and set aside for 15 minutes. Blend breadcrumb mixture, flour, parsley, parmesan and the tablespoon of olive oil in a food processor until well combined. Knead the dough well for 5 minutes, then set aside to rest for 30 minutes.

Preheat oven to 180°C (350°F). Seal the lamb racks in some olive oil in a hot pan for 3–5 minutes. Transfer to a roasting tin and cook in oven for 15 minutes.

Roll out the pasta dough with a rolling pin on a floured board, or with a pasta machine, to a thickness of about 2 mm (⅛ in). Cut into long strips about 1 cm (½ in) wide – these can be rustic (*maltagliatti* means 'roughly cut'). Blanch in a large pan of boiling salted water until all the pasta floats to the surface. Strain and toss with a little olive oil.

To serve, reheat the ragout then stir in the pasta. Add parmesan and butter, stirring gently. Cut the lamb rack at each bone, place a spoonful of ragout and pasta on each plate and arrange a lamb rack on top.

Kiwi **David Matthews** has been cooking in Australia for 12 years – at the Hyatt Adelaide, the National Wine Centre, and at Augé, where he is head chef. **Augé**, 22 Grote Street, Adelaide, South Australia 5000 (08 8410 9332)

SERVES 4

2 tablespoons fennel seeds
2 stalks celery, diced
1 large onion, diced
2 carrots, diced
2 cloves garlic, crushed
olive oil for frying
300 g (10 oz) lamb shoulder,
    boned and diced
2 cups chicken stock
4 lamb racks, with 3 bones on each
4 tablespoons grated parmesan
2 tablespoons butter

PASTA
3 eggs, lightly beaten
125 g (4 oz) dry breadcrumbs
150 g (5 oz) plain (all-purpose) flour
2 tablespoons chopped parsley
2 tablespoons grated parmesan
1 tablespoon olive oil
flour for dusting
a little olive oil

poached king island beef with ginger-soy dipping sauce

Harry Sou, Café China

Pre-order the beef from your butcher. If you can't get King Island beef, any choice beef carpaccio will do. You can make the ginger-soy dipping sauce ahead of time. It will keep in the fridge for a week or two – and goes equally well with pan-fried chicken, pork chops or steamed fish.

For the dipping sauce, heat a little vegetable oil in a wok and sauté garlic and ginger over medium heat until garlic turns golden brown. Add soy sauce and the ¼ cup of chicken stock, then turn heat to low and add sugar. Stir until sugar has dissolved then simmer until the liquid is reduced to about ½ cup. Remove from heat, strain (discarding garlic and ginger) and set aside.

Cook Chinese cabbage until semi-transparent in plenty of lightly salted boiling water with a dash of vegetable oil – about 1–2 minutes. Drain cabbage and arrange in the centre of the serving bowl.

Bring the 4 cups of chicken stock to the boil and poach the beef slices very quickly (20–25 seconds) until medium-rare – they should still be slightly pink. Place beef slices on top of the cabbage, together with sliced ginger, spring onion and capsicum.

In a clean wok, quickly heat 2 tablespoons of vegetable oil over medium heat, then pour oil over the beef and vegetables. Reheat the dipping sauce, drizzle over beef, and garnish with coriander leaves and cracked pepper.

Hong Kong-born **Harry Sou** started his apprenticeship at 15, before coming to Cairns (via the Mask of China restaurant in Melbourne) where, at age 25, he opened his first café. Café China is his fourth restaurant; he opened his fifth, the Café China Noodle Bar, at the Reef Casino – also in Cairns – in 2002.

Café China, Rydges Plaza Shop 12, Spence Street, Cairns, Queensland 4870 (07 4041 2828)

SERVES 4

vegetable oil
2 cloves garlic, finely chopped
2 small slices ginger, julienned
¾ cup light soy sauce
¼ cup chicken stock
2 tablespoons sugar
300 g (10 oz) Chinese cabbage, chopped
4 cups chicken stock
400 g (13 oz) King Island beef carpaccio
1 small knob ginger, sliced
2 spring onions (scallions),
    white parts only, finely sliced
1 medium-sized red capsicum (bell pepper),
    deseeded and sliced
cracked black pepper and coriander
    (cilantro) leaves, to garnish

pan-fried kingfish with jerusalem artichoke purée and watercress sauce

André Chouvin, Feast

For a different twist, add three or four drops of white truffle oil to the artichoke – the two flavours are opposites but very complementary. Clarified butter is butter with the milk solids removed, which means it doesn't burn at high temperatures. You can buy it in cans or tubs at most supermarkets.

Peel the Jerusalem artichokes and slice very thinly. Pan-fry slowly in a tablespoon of butter for 5–10 minutes. When the artichoke starts to soften but before it colours, add the cream. Put a lid on the pan and cook slowly on low heat. When the artichoke is soft (about 8 minutes), purée it, with the cream, in a blender.

Wash the watercress leaves well. Fry the onion in a little butter over medium heat until translucent. Add the watercress leaves, then the fish stock, and cook for 5 minutes (do not cover the pan or the sauce will turn yellow instead of green). Remove from the heat and blend into a purée. Add the 3 tablespoons of butter and stir through.

Heat some clarified butter in a heavy-based frying pan on high heat. Pan-fry the kingfish fillets for a few minutes each side to colour and crisp the outside, then set aside in a warm place to rest for 3 minutes and cook through.

While the fish is resting, gently reheat the artichoke and the sauce. To serve, divide the artichoke evenly between four plates, spoon the watercress sauce around it, and lay a kingfish fillet on top.

André Chouvin trained in France with Paul Bocuse, the Haeberlin brothers and Michel Lorain, later joining Marc Haeberlin at Boston's Julien restaurant. Based in Australia since 1994, André has cultivated award-winning fine dining on the central coast of New South Wales.
Feast, 85 Avoca Drive, Avoca Beach, New South Wales 2251 (02 4381 0707)

SERVES 4

300 g (10 oz) Jerusalem artichokes
butter for frying
100 ml (3 fl oz) cream
$^1/_2$ cup picked watercress leaves
$^1/_2$ onion, diced
$^3/_4$ cup fish stock
3 tablespoons butter
clarified butter for frying
4 kingfish fillets –
   each about 200 g (6 oz) – skin off

jhinga kari (prawn curry)

Louise Harper, Oh! Calcutta!

SERVES 2

4 tablespoons ghee (clarified butter)
1 tablespoon puréed brown onion
2 teaspoons minced garlic
2 teaspoons minced ginger
1 teaspoon ground turmeric
1 teaspoon ground paprika
2 teaspoons ground coriander
250 g (8 oz) uncooked king prawns
    (jumbo shrimp), butterflied
$^2/_3$ cup coconut milk
$^1/_2$ cup water
2 teaspoons tamarind concentrate
$^1/_2$ teaspoon salt
1 small cucumber, cut in half lengthwise,
    deseeded and thinly sliced
1 red onion, thinly sliced
1 long red chilli, deseeded and cut into slivers
small handful torn coriander (cilantro) leaves

This is a deliciously mild curry that will definitely have you coming back for more. Serve it with steamed basmati rice.

Heat ghee in a large frying pan over medium heat and, when hot, fry onion, garlic and ginger. Stir frequently until onions are soft.

Add turmeric, paprika and ground coriander and continue frying for 1 minute. Add prawns and cook, stirring frequently, for about 1 minute. Add coconut milk, water, tamarind and salt and stir well.

When prawns are just cooked and gravy is slightly thickened, serve, garnished with cucumber, red onion, chilli slivers and coriander leaves.

Louise Harper was born in Bombay, the daughter of an Indian naval commander. All her dishes for Oh! Calcutta! are sourced from authentic recipes collected on her regular travels in India, reworked for the Australian palate and climate. She teaches and writes widely about cooking.

Oh! Calcutta!, 251 Victoria Street, Darlinghurst, New South Wales 2010 (02 9360 3650); www.calcutta.citysearch.com.au

chicken breast 'en papillote' with middle-eastern flavours

Peter Brown, Kosta's Taverna

This chicken is great for entertaining because you just put it in the oven for about 40 minutes while you relax with your guests. Use couscous instead of rice, if you prefer.

Mix together all the marinade ingredients, then pour over chicken and refrigerate overnight.

The next day, make the harissa by blending all the ingredients in a food processor until well combined.

Preheat oven to 200°C (400°F). Wrap each chicken breast – together with a generous spoonful of the marinade – in baking paper and tie securely with cooking twine. Bake for 35–40 minutes.

While the chicken is cooking, prepare the pilaf. Bring chicken stock to the boil. In a large, stainless steel saucepan, gently fry onion in olive oil until translucent. Wash rice in a sieve under running water until the water runs clear. Shake off excess water and add rice to onions. Increase heat to medium and stir until rice is heated through and coated with oil. Add garlic and bay leaf, then pour in the boiling stock and stir until it comes back to the boil. Add salt and pepper to taste. Reduce heat, put a tight-fitting lid on the saucepan and simmer gently for 10–15 minutes until all the liquid is absorbed.

Serve the chicken with the pilaf, garnished with a spoonful of harissa, and some coriander leaves and chopped spring onion, if desired.

Peter Brown was trained in the classic European style at Melbourne landmarks such as the Regent Hotel and Haggar's. He has been chef at the Mediterranean-style Kosta's Taverna in Lorne since 2001.

Kosta's Taverna, 48 Mountjoy Parade, Lorne, Victoria 3232 (03 5289 1883)

SERVES 6

6 plump free-range chicken breasts on
   the bone – each about 250 g (8 oz)
fresh coriander (cilantro) leaves, to garnish
4 spring onions (scallions), chopped, to garnish

MARINADE
1½ tablespoons Pernod
juice and finely grated zest of 1 lime
2 tablespoons olive oil
1 tablespoon honey
1 knob fresh ginger, grated
2 cloves garlic, finely chopped
1 teaspoon ground cumin
1 teaspoon cayenne pepper
1 teaspoon ground cinnamon
3 teaspoons Dijon mustard
6 stalks fresh coriander (cilantro)
½ cup pistachio nuts, chopped
salt and pepper

HARISSA
125 g (4 oz) bird's eye chillies, seeds removed
3 cloves garlic, roughly chopped
2 cups fresh coriander (cilantro) leaves
1 teaspoon caraway seeds, roasted and ground
1 teaspoon coriander seeds, roasted and ground
½ cup olive oil
2 teaspoons tomato paste

PILAF
5 cups chicken stock
1 large brown onion, finely diced
½ cup olive oil
2 cups basmati rice
1 clove garlic, finely chopped
1 bay leaf
salt and pepper

slow-cooked ocean trout with seaweed and spinach horseradish sauce

Serge Dansereau, The Bathers' Pavilion

I love ocean trout cooked in this way – it has a great texture, a perfect balance of fat and silkiness, and a very refined flavour.

Sprinkle the trout fillets with shredded nori and wrap in cling film. Chill until ready to cook.

Preheat oven to 180°C (350°F). Wrap the garlic in foil, together with a little of the butter and the sprig of thyme. Roast for 15 minutes, then set aside to cool. Turn down the oven to its minimum setting – about 120°C (250°F).

Blanch 1 kg (2 lb) of the baby spinach in boiling water. Drain and, while it's still hot, purée with the unsalted butter and the roasted garlic (just squeeze the garlic out of its papery skin). Season with salt and pepper. Blanch the remaining 500 g (1 lb) of baby spinach, refresh in iced water and squeeze dry. Finely chop and add to the puréed spinach. Soak the dried wakame in cold water until it is reconstituted and soft. Squeeze dry, chop and add to the spinach purée.

Blend the horseradish with the vinegar and sugar. Gradually add the oil until you have an emulsified sauce the consistency of a thick cream soup. Taste, adjust the salt, and add a little wasabi if more heat is required.

To cook the trout, place wrapped fish portions in an open oven on the minimum setting. Cook for 20 minutes, rotating every 5 minutes to ensure even cooking. By this time the fish should be cooked, but still soft and retaining its natural colour.

Meanwhile, sauté the parsnips in butter until tender.

Heat the spinach and place in the centre of each plate, drizzle the horseradish sauce around the spinach, arrange the parsnips on the sauce and place the unwrapped trout on top. Sprinkle with sea salt flakes and serve.

Montreal-born **Serge Dansereau** was lured to Sydney to launch the Regent Hotel in 1983. He steered its signature restaurant, Kables, to stellar levels and was subsequently lauded by the *Sydney Morning Herald Good Food Guide* for 'helping redefine Australian cuisine', a quest he continues at The Bathers' Pavilion.
The Bathers' Pavilion, 4 The Esplanade, Balmoral Beach, New South Wales 2088 (02 9969 5050)

SERVES 8

8 × 185 g (6 oz) fillets ocean trout, skin and pin bones removed
2/3 cup shredded nori seaweed
5 cloves garlic, unpeeled
125 g (4 oz) unsalted butter
sprig of thyme
1.5 kg (3 lb) baby spinach
90 g (3 oz) dried wakame seaweed
salt and pepper
155 g (5 oz) fresh horseradish, peeled and finely grated – if unavailable, substitute pickled horseradish
3/4 cup white wine vinegar
3 tablespoons white sugar
2 cups grape seed oil
wasabi paste, if desired
5 parsnips, cut into 1 cm (1/2 in) dice
butter for frying
sea salt flakes

john dory with whitebait fritter, roast tomatoes and sauce gribiche

Angel Fernandez, Catalina

SERVES 6

³/₄ cup plain (all-purpose) flour

1¹/₂ cups grated parmesan

3 eggs

400 g (13 oz) New Zealand whitebait
(nanata or Chinese silver fish)

¹/₂ cup chopped chives

salt and pepper

100 ml (3 fl oz) vegetable oil

6 vine-ripened tomatoes

100 ml (3 fl oz) extra virgin olive oil

6 John Dory fillets – each 160–180 g (5–6 oz)
– skin removed

juice of 1 lemon

SAUCE

250 ml (8 fl oz) good thick mayonnaise

1 hard-boiled egg, roughly grated

¹/₂ cup cornichons (small gherkins),
finely chopped

2 tablespoons salted capers, washed
and finely chopped

1 tablespoon chopped flat-leaf parsley

1 tablespoon chopped tarragon

1 tablespoon chopped chives

salt and pepper

Make the whitebait fritters large enough to cover the fish. When diners lift the fritter, they'll be surprised by all the treasures underneath.

Mix all the sauce ingredients together, add some pepper and check for salt – you might not need it as capers are quite salty.

To make the fritters, combine flour and parmesan in a bowl and slowly whisk in the eggs, one at a time. Beat until it forms a smooth, thick batter. Fold in white-bait and chives until well combined. Season, then fry a little bit in vegetable oil, taste to check the seasoning, and adjust as necessary. Place batter in fridge until required.

Preheat oven to 200°C (400°F). Cut tomatoes in half and place on a baking tray in the oven with some olive oil, salt and pepper and roast for about 15 minutes, until tomatoes have softened but still hold their shape.

Meanwhile, pour a little vegetable oil into a large frying pan over medium–high heat. Season the John Dory fillets with salt and pepper and, when the oil is almost at smoking point, sear fillets on one side until golden brown. Remove from pan and place raw-side down on an oiled baking tray. Set aside.

Add a little more vegetable oil to the pan and wait until it heats up again. Ladle the whitebait batter into pan, forming six large fritters each big enough to cover a Dory fillet. You may need to do this in two or more batches, depending on the size of your frying pan. Fry until golden, then flip over and cook for another 30 seconds. Place a fritter on top of each fish fillet, then put the fritter-topped fish in the oven for 5 minutes.

To serve, spoon a dollop of sauce onto each plate, top with two roasted tomato halves and arrange a fritter-topped fish fillet so that it covers tomatoes and sauce. Drizzle with a little extra virgin olive oil and lemon juice and serve immediately.

Chilean **Angel Fernandez** was inspired by the cooking of his caterer grand-mother. 'I fell in love with food,' he recalls. After his family migrated to Australia in 1986 he landed a job with Neil Perry's Rockpool group. He started at Sydney's Catalina restaurant in 1995 and is now head chef.

Catalina, 1 Sunderland Avenue, Rose Bay, New South Wales 2029 (02 9371 0555); www.catalinarosebay.com.au

'naked ravioli' with sage butter

Robert Castellani, Donovans

SERVES 6–8

750 g (1½ lb) fresh spinach
750 g (1½ lb) silver beet (Swiss chard)
500 g (1 lb) ricotta
5 egg yolks
2 cups finely grated parmesan
coarse-grained sea salt and freshly ground
    black pepper
½ teaspoon grated nutmeg
1 cup plain (all-purpose) flour
1 tablespoon butter
12–16 sage leaves
shaved parmesan, to serve

The title is a little cheeky. It's a play on words, as these are really gnocchi, but you can also use the mixture as a filling for ravioli or cannelloni.

Blanch the spinach and silver beet leaves for 5 minutes in boiling water. Refresh in cold water, then chop finely. Remove excess water from the ricotta by wrapping it tightly in a clean tea towel and squeezing it.

In a bowl, mix the spinach and silver beet with the ricotta, egg yolks and grated parmesan. Season with salt and pepper and add the nutmeg. When thoroughly combined, form the ricotta mix into walnut-sized balls and roll lightly in the flour, making sure all the gnocchi are uniformly floured.

Bring a large pan of salted water to the boil and poach the gnocchi for 30 seconds.

Heat the butter in a warm pan until it starts to foam, then add the sage leaves. Toss the gnocchi quickly in the sage butter, then divide between six or eight warmed shallow bowls. Garnish with parmesan shavings and serve immediately.

Robert Castellani was born in Lombardy, Italy. He commenced his apprenticeship in Melbourne at Fanny's before moving to Stephanie's, where he worked for 7 years, 5 of those as head chef. In 1996 he joined Gail and Kevin Donovan at their restaurant, Donovans, in the Melbourne bayside suburb of St Kilda; Robert also accompanied Gail and Kevin on their travels in southern Italy that culminated in the publication of *Saluté!*, which won best hardcover food book at the World Food Media Awards in 2001.

Donovans, 40 Jacka Boulevard, St Kilda, Victoria 3182 (03 9534 8221); www.donovanshouse.com.au

St Kilda, Victoria

chilli calamari and blue swimmer crab spaghettini with bisque cream sauce

Glen Barratt, Armstrong's

Be careful not to overcook the calamari, otherwise it will become rubbery and unappetising.

Shell crabs, reserving shells for the sauce. Clean calamari and slice tubes into rounds.

Mix finely sliced shallot with calamari and sambal oelek, then set aside to marinate in the refrigerator.

Blanch tomatoes briefly in boiling water then peel, deseed and dice them. Combine with the finely diced shallot, garlic, extra virgin olive oil and sliced parsley to make a simple salsa. Season with pepper and salt and set aside.

For the sauce, sauté onion, carrot, lemongrass and reserved crab shells in a pan with a little olive oil until the onion is well caramelised. Add tomato or pasta sauce, wine and chicken stock, and stir to deglaze the pan. Reduce by half and add cream. Simmer for 10 minutes then add parsley, marjoram and Pernod. Add arrowroot paste to thicken, season to taste, then pass through a sieve. Keep warm.

Bring a pot of salted water to the boil, add a few drops of oil and cook the spaghettini until 'al dente'.

Meanwhile, put a large frying pan over high heat and add a little olive oil. When the oil starts to smoke, sear calamari for 10–15 seconds. Quickly add crab, shake pan, then remove calamari and crab. Deglaze pan with wine and chicken stock. Reduce liquid by three-quarters then add drained spaghettini. Toss in lemon juice and zest and tomato salsa, then gently stir through calamari and crab. Season and serve immediately, with the hot bisque cream sauce poured over and garnished with parsley.

Glen Barratt has worked at notable Australian restaurants such as Chevaliers and Tables of Toowong, where he met master chef Russell Armstrong. He has been head chef at Armstrong's in Brisbane since 1999.
Armstrong's, 73 Wickham Terrace, Brisbane, Queensland 4000 (07 3832 4566)

SERVES 4

2 cooked blue swimmer or sand crabs
400 g (13 oz) baby calamari
1 golden shallot, finely sliced
2 tablespoons sambal oelek
   (mild Indonesian chilli paste)
4 ripe tomatoes
1 golden shallot, finely diced
1 small clove garlic, minced
1/3 cup extra virgin olive oil
3 tablespoons finely sliced flat-leaf parsley
salt and ground white pepper
olive oil for frying
350 ml (11 fl oz) dry white wine
350 ml (11 fl oz) chicken stock
200 g (6½ oz) spaghettini
juice and finely grated zest of ½ lemon
flat-leaf parsley sprigs, to garnish

SAUCE

1 small onion, diced
1 small carrot, diced
2 stalks lemongrass
a little olive oil
1 cup homemade tomato sauce or
   good-quality bottled pasta sauce
1 cup dry white wine
2 cups chicken stock
2 cups cream
2 teaspoons chopped flat-leaf parsley
2 teaspoons chopped sweet marjoram
1 tablespoon Pernod
1 teaspoon arrowroot, mixed to a paste
   with a little cold water

smoked salmon parcels with salmon roe salsa and lemon vinaigrette

Ben Sharp and Bernard Oehrli, The Manse

SERVES 4

400 g (13 oz) smoked salmon –
    ideally Tasmanian
8 chive batons

POTATO SALAD FILLING
500 g (1 lb) kipfler potatoes
10 golden shallots, diced
3 tablespoons chopped parsley
30 g (1 oz) baby capers, washed
100 g (3½ oz) prepared horseradish
2 tablespoons seeded mustard mayonnaise
2 tablespoons crème fraîche
sea salt and ground white pepper

SALSA
¼ large cucumber, deseeded and finely diced
4 tomatoes, quartered, deseeded
    and finely diced
6–8 spring onions (scallions), finely chopped
3 tablespoons chopped chives
1 apple, cored and finely diced – a tart
    Granny Smith works well
150 g (5 oz) salmon roe – ideally Yarra Valley
squeeze of lemon juice
dash of olive oil

LEMON VINAIGRETTE
juice of 2 lemons
1 tablespoon Dijon mustard
100 ml (3 fl oz) vegetable oil
100 ml (3 fl oz) olive oil
2 egg yolks
salt and ground white pepper
1 teaspoon caster (superfine) sugar

Pack the salmon parcels tight by firmly pushing in the potato salad and you will get beautifully symmetrical parcels.

To make the potato salad filling, put the potatoes in plenty of cold salted water and bring to the boil. Simmer until you can press the tip of a small knife into them without resistance. Cool, uncovered, in the refrigerator. When cool, peel the potatoes and cut into 1 cm (½ in) dice. Add the shallots, parsley, capers, horseradish, mayonnaise and crème fraiche. Mix together well and season with salt and pepper.

Line the bottom and sides of four round moulds – 5cm (2 in) diameter by 7 cm (3 in) high – with the smoked salmon and pack tightly with potato salad. Cover with more salmon, then wrap tightly in cling film to prevent the salmon from drying out. Place the salmon parcels in the refrigerator.

For the salsa, combine all the ingredients, adding just enough olive oil to give a shiny glazed appearance.

To make the vinaigrette, blend the lemon juice, mustard, vegetable and olive oils and egg yolks in a blender until the dressing turns white and thickens. Season with salt, pepper and sugar to achieve a balance of sweet and sour.

To serve, pour a perfect circle of vinaigrette in the centre of each of four white plates. Ease a salmon parcel out of its mould and place in the vinaigrette. Place a teaspoonful of the salsa on top, and garnish with two chive batons.

Ben Sharp worked at restaurants in South Australia and Queensland before settling in under mentor Bernard Oehrli at The Manse, in Adelaide. He describes his food as 'classical techniques that don't mess around with trendy flavours'. Swiss-born and -trained, **Bernard Oehrli** worked in five-star hotels in Switzerland, Bermuda, Egypt and the Pacific before taking over The Manse in 1993.
The Manse Restaurant, 142 Tynte Street, North Adelaide, South Australia 5006 (08 8267 4636); www.manserestaurant.com.au

vitello alla buon ricordo

Armando Percuoco, Buon Ricordo

This is a traditional Italian recipe that's usually made with pork, but I have re-created it with the veal because it is much lighter for the Australian palate and climate.

First, make the croquettes. Boil the potatoes with their skins on. When cooked, drain, peel and mash the potatoes, then mix in the parmesan, butter and parsley. Season with salt and pepper. Shape the potato mixture into narrow oblongs about 7 × 2 cm (3 × 1 in). Roll the croquettes in flour, dip evenly in egg white then dust with breadcrumbs. Deep-fry the croquettes in olive oil until golden. Drain on kitchen paper then transfer to a baking tray.

Preheat oven to 200°C (400°F). Slice the veal into four pieces then pound very flat with a mallet or meat tenderiser. Beat the eggs until fluffy and season with a little salt and pepper. Add the chopped rosemary and mix well. Smear the egg mixture over the top of each veal slice, then top with three slices of pancetta and two slices of smoked cheese. Roll and tie with string to secure. Heat the olive oil in a heavy, ovenproof pan and quickly brown the meat for a minute or two only. Transfer pan to oven and cook the veal for 10 minutes, then remove and let rest for 3 minutes. While the veal is resting and you're making the sauce, place the croquettes in the oven to warm through.

For the sauce, deglaze the veal pan on top of the stove with wine and butter, reducing the liquid until you have a dense sauce. Season with salt and pepper, if necessary.

Slice the veal into medallions and divide between four plates. Pour the sauce over the meat and accompany with croquettes.

Armando Percuoco comes from a family of restaurateurs whose roots date back to post-war Naples. He started working for his father, Mario, at Le Arcate, one of the top restaurants in Naples. In 1972, he emigrated to Australia, and in 1979 he and his father opened Pulcinella in Sydney's Kings Cross. Buon Ricordo opened in Paddington in 1987, and remains one of Australia's finest Italian restaurants.
Buon Ricordo, 108 Boundary Street, Paddington, New South Wales 2021 (02 9360 6729)

SERVES 4

400 g (13 oz) veal backstrap
2 eggs
salt and pepper
2 tablespoons chopped rosemary
12 thin slices pancetta, prosciutto or bacon
8 thin slices smoked provola
    or smoked mozzarella
olive oil for frying
1½ cups white wine
1 tablespoon butter

CROQUETTES
5 medium-sized potatoes
2 tablespoons grated parmesan
1 tablespoon butter
1 tablespoon chopped flat-leaf parsley
salt and pepper
1 cup plain (all-purpose) flour for dusting
1 egg white, lightly beaten
1 cup dried breadcrumbs
olive oil for deep-frying

tortelloni of fish with a champagne and cucumber froth

Gavin Opie, Beaumaris Pavilion

Make sure all your ingredients are as fresh as possible – the freshness is what makes the difference.

First, make the tortelloni. Place the flour and salt for the white and black tortellini in separate bowls and make a well in the centre. For the white tortelloni, add eggs, egg yolks and oil and combine until you have a smooth dough. For the black tortelloni, blend squid ink with eggs and strain before mixing with yolks and olive oil, then add liquid to flour and combine until you have a smooth dough. Let the dough for both pastas rest for 1 hour.

Meanwhile, make the tortelloni filling and the caramelised witlof. For the tortelloni filling, mince trevally and blue eye in a food processor. Mix in egg whites, being careful not to overwork. Transfer to a bowl and add cream, mixing with a wooden spoon or plastic spatula. Add crabmeat and herbs, and season to taste.

For the witlof, preheat oven to 200°C (400°F). Brown witlof in a frying pan in a little oil, adding butter and sugar to caramelise. Transfer to a baking dish, pour over the warm chicken stock, cover and cook for 15 minutes in oven.

While the witlof is cooking, make the sauce. Peel and roughly chop cucumber. Simmer shallots, mushrooms, thyme, white wine, champagne and fish stock for about 15–20 minutes, until reduced to a jam-like consistency. Transfer to a clean pan and add cream. Reduce this over medium heat for several minutes, until it becomes sticky. Add lemon juice, seasoning and cucumber pulp. Allow the flavour of the cucumber to infuse the sauce for a few minutes before straining. Keep the sauce warm while you prepare the tortelloni.

Roll out both pasta doughs with a pasta machine (or with a rolling pin on a floured surface) to 3 mm (⅛ in) thick, then cut out twelve 10 cm (4 in) rounds from each colour. Place two teaspoons of the filling in the centre of each disc then fold dough in half, keeping the filling in the centre. Press edges to form a seal and bring the two ends together in a ring to form tortelloni. Shape and squeeze together. Heat a large pan of salted water to boiling point, add tortelloni and simmer gently for about 3 minutes, until 'al dente'.

Blanch julienned leek in boiling water. Sear scallops quickly on a hot chargrill in a little olive oil for about 20 seconds each side.

SERVES 4

50 g (2 oz) witlof (Belgian endive)
olive oil for frying
½ tablespoon butter
1 teaspoon sugar
¼ cup warm chicken stock
1 tablespoon julienned leek, white part only
4 sea scallops
1 tablespoon snipped chives

WHITE TORTELLONI
220 g (7 oz) plain (all-purpose) flour
2 eggs
2 egg yolks
1½ teaspoons olive oil
½ teaspoon salt

BLACK TORTELLONI
220 g (7 oz) plain (all-purpose) flour
2 eggs
2 egg yolks
1 teaspoon olive oil
½ teaspoon squid ink
½ teaspoon salt

TORTELLONI FILLING
100 g (3 oz) trevally fillet, skin and bones removed
100 g (3 oz) blue eye fillet, skin and bones removed
2 egg whites
30 ml (1 fl oz) cream
20 g (1 oz) picked crabmeat
2 tablespoons chopped herbs – dill, chives, chervil
salt and pepper

SAUCE

¹/₂ small cucumber
2 golden shallots, finely sliced
2 button mushrooms, finely sliced
small sprig thyme
1 cup white wine
¹/₂ cup champagne
1 cup fish stock
1 cup cream
squeeze of lemon juice
salt and pepper

To serve, place some caramelised witlof in the centre of each bowl. Arrange three black and three white tortelloni on top, draped with the leek strands. Place a warm scallop on top of each black tortelloni, pour over the hot champagne sauce and garnish with chives.

Originally from New Zealand, **Gavin Opie** has been head chef at the well-known Melbourne restaurants Stella and Walter's Wine Bar, and now heads the kitchen at the Beaumaris Pavilion.

Beaumaris Pavilion, 472 Beach Road, Beaumaris, Victoria 3193 (03 9589 3251); www.beaumarispavilion.com.au

Brighton Beach, Victoria

slow-braised beef brisket

Mark Best, Marque

A remarkably simple and versatile dish whose only requirement, as with all good cooking, is that you choose the best produce. Look for a fine piece of brisket – grain-fed Angus or, even better, Wagyu beef – and serve with vegetables, such as sweet and sour turnips or roasted globe artichokes. Put the brisket in the oven before you set off on a wintry walk by the ocean and you'll come back to a hearty, warming dinner.

Place the brisket in a casserole just large enough to hold it. Add carrot, onion, celery, herbs, spices and garlic. If the stock has jellied, melt it in a pan over low heat, then pour over the meat. Cover the casserole with a tight-fitting lid or cling film, set the oven to its minimum setting – about 100–120°C (210–250°F) – and cook for 7–8 hours. When cooked, the meat will be easily pierced with a skewer. The beef can be prepared up to this point a day ahead.

When ready to serve, heat the oven to 180°C (350°F). Drain the meat and strain the stock. Place the meat in a large roasting tin and add 2 cups of the stock. Place in the oven and, about every 5 minutes, baste the brisket with the stock until a glaze forms on the meat – this should take about 30 minutes.

Pour the rest of the stock into a pan and reduce by half over medium heat. Serve alongside the meat as a sauce.

Mark Best worked under renowned French chefs Alain Passard and Raymond Blanc before opening his fêted French restaurant, Marque, in Sydney.
Marque, 355 Crown Street, Surry Hills, New South Wales 2010 (02 9332 2225)

SERVES 4–6

2 kg (4 lb) point end of grain-fed beef brisket
1 large carrot, cut into chunks
1 large onion, cut into wedges
1 stalk celery, cut into lengths
sprig of thyme
3 bay leaves – ideally fresh
4 star anise
1 teaspoon white peppercorns
1 teaspoon coriander seeds
1 head of garlic, cut in half horizontally
4 cups veal or beef stock

dana kulbasti (chargrilled veal with eggplant, spinach and lemon dressing)

Serif Kaya, Ottoman Cuisine

SERVES 4

1 large eggplant (aubergine)
salt
400 g (13 oz) veal backstrap
freshly ground black pepper
2 tablespoons crushed medium-hot
   dried chillies
1 tablespoon fresh oregano
pinch of sugar
olive oil for grilling
plain (all-purpose) flour and vegetable oil
   for coating meat
1 cup chicken stock
juice of 2 medium lemons
90 g (3 oz) baby spinach leaves
cracked pepper
knob butter
sumac, to garnish

LEMON DRESSING
juice of 2 medium lemons
1 teaspoon Dijon mustard
½ cup olive oil
salt, pepper and sugar to taste

This is one of the most popular dishes at Ottoman, and a favourite of Dame Edna Everage (aka Barry Humphries). We generally serve this with a rice dish, such as pilaf.

Cut eggplant into thin slices, sprinkle with salt, and set aside to draw out any bitter juices. Slice the veal backstrap thinly and season both sides of the slices with salt, pepper and crushed chilli to taste. Cover and refrigerate for at least 1–2 hours, or overnight (in the restaurant, we like to prepare the meat a day in advance).

Rinse eggplant slices, pat dry and season lightly with oregano and a pinch of sugar to neutralise any remaining bitterness. Brush eggplant slices with olive oil, then barbecue or chargrill over a high heat until golden brown on both sides, brushing with more oil as required. Set aside.

Prepare two trays or plates large enough for dipping the veal slices: pour a thin layer of flour into one, and vegetable oil into the other. Also prepare a small bowl or cup of chicken stock seasoned with lemon juice and a little olive oil.

For the dressing, whisk or blend lemon juice, mustard and oil together until well combined. Add seasoning to taste.

Blanch spinach leaves in boiling water until wilted; drain and toss with cracked pepper and a knob of butter. Keep warm while you cook the meat.

Remove veal from refrigerator and coat slices with flour then oil, allowing excess oil to drain onto the tray or plate before placing veal on a hot chargrill or barbecue. The oil should cause the veal to flame and seal. Cook for 30–40 seconds per side, brushing each side once with the seasoned chicken stock to keep the meat juicy. When all the veal is cooked, return eggplant briefly to the grill to reheat.

Pile three or four veal slices on each plate and top with spinach and eggplant. Sprinkle sumac on top, then lightly drizzle with lemon dressing.

Born in Turkey, **Serif Kaya** worked his way across the kitchens of Europe before coming to Australia in 1980. He opened the award-winning Ottoman Cuisine in Canberra in 1992, where he serves traditional Ottoman dishes cooked the way he would like to eat them.

Ottoman Cuisine, 9 Broughton Street (cnr Blackall Street), Barton, Australian Capital Territory 2600 (02 6273 6111)

prawn and scampi risotto

James Kidman, Otto

We use vialone nano rice because it can withstand a bit of overcooking. If scampi is unavailable, you can substitute crabmeat.

To make stock, heat oil in a heavy-based saucepan over medium heat and add carrot, celery, leek, onion and garlic. Turn heat to low and sauté until lightly caramelised. Add tomato paste and cook for a further 2 minutes. Add prawn shells, scampi heads and fennel stalks and cook for a further 5 minutes. Add 4 litres (16 cups) of water and bring to the boil. Simmer for 1½ hours, periodically skimming impurities. Strain through a fine sieve, return to saucepan and keep at a gentle simmer.

To cook the risotto, heat olive oil in a saucepan and add onion, celery, leek and garlic. Cook over low heat without allowing the vegetables to colour. Add rice and cook for 2–3 minutes, then add vermouth and stir until absorbed. Add simmering stock one ladle at a time, stirring continuously until the rice grains are plump and creamy. This should take about 20 minutes. Just before serving, add prawn meat (it will cook through in the residual heat), peas, lemon zest, chopped fennel and butter. Work the risotto hard with a wooden spoon to make it really creamy, then season with salt and pepper.

Brush a little olive oil over the scampi halves, season lightly with sea salt and grill for 1 minute. Spoon the risotto into each of six bowls and place three grilled scampi halves on top.

After training with some of Australia's best-known chefs, **James Kidman** became head chef at Otto in 2002. 'Italian cooking fits into my persona,' he says. 'It's pretty relaxed and simple.'

Otto, Area 8/6 Cowper Wharf Road, Woolloomooloo, New South Wales 2011 (02 9368 7488)

SERVES 6

4 tablespoons olive oil
1 onion, finely diced
1 stalk celery, finely diced
1 leek, finely diced
2 cloves garlic, crushed
300 g (10 oz) risotto rice – vialone nano
   or arborio
150 ml (5 fl oz) dry vermouth
300 g (10 oz) uncooked prawns (shrimp),
   peeled, deveined and roughly chopped into
   thirds – retain shells and heads for stock
150 g (5 oz) fresh or frozen green peas
finely grated zest of 1 lemon
2 tablespoons chopped fennel herb –
   reserve stalks for stock
100 g (3 oz) unsalted butter
sea salt and pepper
9 scampi, heads removed and tails halved
   lengthwise – retain heads for stock

STOCK

3 tablespoons olive oil
1 carrot, roughly chopped
1 stalk celery, roughly chopped
1 leek, roughly chopped
1 onion, roughly chopped
2 cloves garlic, roughly chopped
1 tablespoon tomato paste
prawn (shrimp) shells and scampi heads
fennel herb stalks

Woolloomooloo, New South Wales

livebait paella
Cath Claringbold, mecca

The first time I tasted paella I was hooked: masses of fresh fish and seafood and the very best of Spanish flavours, from smoky paprika to spicy chorizo, all with a hearty rustic charm. This version is the one served at Livebait, mecca's sister restaurant in Melbourne's Docklands.

Place a 28 cm (11 in) paella pan or frying pan over medium–high heat and throw in the sliced chorizo – it will release some of its own oil and colour slightly. Add the prawns and fry briefly, but do not cook all the way through. Remove the prawns and chorizo and set aside.

Add a little olive oil to the pan and fry the onion and capsicum for 15–20 minutes, stirring frequently. Add the garlic and fennel seeds and cook until the vegetables are sweet and completely soft.

Meanwhile, put the chicken stock in a saucepan, add the saffron and bring to the boil.

Add the rice to the paella pan and mix well. Increase the heat and add the white wine, followed by the hot stock. Add smoked paprika and season well with salt and pepper. From this point on, do not stir the rice, just gently shake the pan from time to time to stop the rice from catching.

Turn the heat down to a simmer and cook for about 15 minutes, then return the chorizo and prawns to the pan and allow to cook until the liquid has been absorbed and the rice is almost cooked.

Cover the pan tightly with foil and allow to rest for about 5 minutes before serving. To serve, sprinkle with loads of freshly chopped parsley, and lemon wedges.

Cath Claringbold trained with some of Australia's finest chefs – Stephanie Alexander, Jacques Reymond and Greg Malouf – before becoming executive chef at mecca in Melbourne.

mecca, Mid-level Southgate, 3 Southgate Avenue, Southbank, Victoria 3006 (03 9682 2999); www.mecca.net.au

SERVES 4

150 g (5 oz) chorizo sausage, thickly sliced
8 uncooked king prawns (jumbo shrimp),
    peeled and deveined but with tails intact
olive oil for frying
2 red onions, finely chopped
1 green capsicum (bell pepper),
    cut into large dice
4 cloves garlic, finely chopped
½ teaspoon fennel seeds
3 cups chicken stock
pinch saffron threads
250 g (8 oz) paella rice – I prefer
    Calasparra brand
⅓ cup dry white wine
½ teaspoon smoked paprika
salt and freshly ground black pepper
freshly chopped flat-leaf parsley
lemon wedges

roast boned saddle of lamb with tomato confit, kipfler potato, shallots and garlic

Dean Sammut, Artespresso

SERVES 4

4 roma (plum) tomatoes
salt and pepper
100 ml (3 fl oz) olive oil
1 lamb saddle – about 1–1.2 kg (2–2½ lb)
14 cloves garlic, peeled
1 tablespoon picked thyme leaves
1 tablespoon picked oregano leaves
2–3 tablespoons picked flat-leaf parsley leaves
finely grated zest of 1 lemon
60 g (2 oz) parmesan, grated
12 golden shallots, peeled
1 tablespoon vegetable oil
3 tablespoons butter
6 kipfler potatoes
200 ml (6 fl oz) good brown stock
2 anchovy fillets, finely chopped

Tell your butcher you want the saddle from a young lamb – preferably one that weighed 15–18 kilos (about 30–36 lb), otherwise it will be too large. Ask for the saddle to be deboned, reserving the fillet. You could also make this recipe with racks of lamb.

Cut the tomatoes in half and place cut-side down on a baking tray sprinkled with salt and pepper. Pour the olive oil over and place the tray in a very slow oven – 100°C (210°F) – for 3–4 hours, or until the tomatoes are soft but still holding their shape. Remove the tomatoes and turn up the oven to 210°C (425°F).

Remove the belly flap from the boned saddle, leaving just 1 cm (½ in) on either side of the loin. Place the fillet in this 'pocket' between the two loins. Chop two of the garlic cloves. In a bowl, mix the chopped garlic with all the herbs, plus the lemon zest and parmesan. Season the lamb with salt and pepper and liberally sprinkle with the herb mixture. Roll up and tie with string.

In a small pan, gently fry the shallots and the remaining twelve garlic cloves in vegetable oil and butter over a low heat until golden brown and very well cooked.

Steam the potatoes until cooked – about 15–20 minutes – then peel and slice. While the potatoes are cooking, place the lamb on a roasting tin and roast for about 15 minutes until medium. Let stand in a warm place for 5 minutes before carving.

Pour the stock into a large pan, add the tomatoes, potatoes, shallots, garlic and anchovy, and simmer until the liquid is reduced to a sauce-like consistency. Divide the vegetables between four plates. Carve the lamb into slices about 1.5 cm (¾ in) thick and arrange on top of the vegetables. Pour the sauce over and serve immediately.

Dean Sammut trained with Serge Dansereau in Sydney then headed to Europe, where he worked with the Roux brothers at Le Gavroche. Back in Sydney he cooked at the legendary Darley Street Thai with David Thompson.

Artespresso, 31 Giles Street, Kingston, Australian Capital Territory 2604 (02 6295 8055); www.artespresso.com.au

pan-seared ocean trout with broccolini and corn in yellow thai curry broth

Girard Ramsay, Grange Jetty Kiosk

Any leftover sauce from this dish can be tossed through some cooked noodles, vegetables and bean sprouts to make a light lunch.

Preheat oven to 200°C (400°F).

In a medium-sized pan, gently sauté onion and ginger in some vegetable oil until translucent. Add chillies, palm sugar, coconut milk, turmeric and curry powder. Bring to a simmer and add corn kernels. Adjust seasoning with lime juice and fish sauce, but use sparingly, as too much of either will ruin the dish. Add bean sprouts to curry and allow to simmer for 1 minute to cook through. Take off the heat, cover and keep warm.

Heat a non-stick frying pan, add 2–3 tablespoons of vegetable oil and sear the fish over medium heat for 90 seconds each side. Remove fish from pan and place in oven for 3–4 minutes for a medium-cooked fillet.

Blanch broccolini or broccoli in boiling water for 2 minutes, drain and keep warm.

To serve, pour the yellow curry into four bowls. Place two broccolini or a few florets of broccoli in each bowl, lay the fish on top and garnish with coriander leaves.

Canadian-born **Girard Ramsay** began his career in Saskatoon, Saskatchewan, worked at various award-winning restaurants in Vancouver, and came to South Australia and the Grange Jetty Kiosk in 2001.

Grange Jetty Kiosk, cnr Jetty Road and Esplanade, Grange, South Australia 5022 (08 8235 0822)

SERVES 4

1 medium white onion, sliced
1 small knob ginger, finely chopped
vegetable oil for frying
2 red bird's eye chillies, deseeded
   and finely chopped
1 teaspoon grated palm sugar
2 × 400 ml (13 fl oz) tins coconut milk
½ teaspoon ground turmeric
½ teaspoon curry powder
3 cobs corn, washed and kernels trimmed
   from cob *or* 1 × 400 g (13 oz) tin corn
   kernels, drained
splash of lime juice
splash of fish sauce
200 g (6 oz) bean sprouts
4 × 200 g (6 oz) fillets of ocean trout
   or salmon
8 pieces broccolini *or* 1 cup broccoli florets,
   trimmed and washed
1 cup coriander (cilantro) leaves

french lamb cutlets

Osamu Uchino, Absolutely chez Uchino

SERVES 4

¼ leek
½ brown onion
1 medium-sized carrot
1 stalk celery
knob of butter
500 g (1 lb) minced veal
2 egg whites
100 ml (3 fl oz) cream
salt, pepper and ground nutmeg
12 lamb cutlets
1 cup dried white breadcrumbs
vegetable oil for frying

This lovely recipe is great for a casual weekend lunch or dinner. Serve with roast potatoes or a selection of roast vegetables.

Finely dice the leek, onion, carrot and celery. Melt the butter in a frying pan and sauté the vegetables until soft and translucent. Put the veal mince and egg whites in a food processor and process until firm (1–2 minutes). With the motor running, slowly add the cream, then season to taste with salt, pepper and nutmeg. Add the sautéed vegetables and pulse for 10–20 seconds just to soften the stuffing, being careful not to overwork the mixture.

Preheat oven to 200°C (400°F). Using a dessertspoon, coat the cutlets with the stuffing. Spread breadcrumbs on a tray or plate and roll the cutlets in the crumbs until they are well coated. Heat a generous amount of oil in a frying pan and lightly brown each cutlet on both sides, then place in the oven for about 10 minutes, until still pink in the middle.

Osamu Uchino was born in Japan and honed his skills in European cuisine at numerous five-star hotels in Japan, Europe, Chicago and New York. In 1990 he opened the landmark Perth restaurant, Chez Uchino. In 2002 Osamu opened Absolutely chez Uchino, a gourmet takeaway restaurant.

Absolutely chez Uchino, 622 Sterling Highway, Mosman Park, Western Australia 6012 (08 9385 2202)

roast wild barramundi fillet with shellfish fricassee and saffron vegetable broth

Michael Lambie, Circa, The Prince

It's important not to cook the yabbies or crayfish for too long, otherwise the flesh goes dry and rubbery. It should be just very lightly poached for about 45 seconds.

Preheat oven to 200°C (400°F).

Heat the stock to a gentle simmer and briefly poach the yabbies (for about 45 seconds) and scallops (for about 20 seconds).

In a large pan, sweat half of the diced carrot and celery and the saffron in 3 tablespoons of the olive oil over medium heat for 2 minutes, then quickly add the mussels and clams. Add the white wine and cook, covered, over high heat until the shells open. Remove the mussels and clams and reserve the cooking liquid. Shuck the oysters, if necessary.

Place 3 tablespoons of the olive oil in a baking dish and put in oven until the oil starts to smoke – about 1 minute. Place the barramundi fillets in the oil, skin-side down, and roast for 4 minutes.

Bring the reserved cooking liquid to the boil and add all the shellfish. Stir in the tomatoes, parsley and the remaining diced vegetables, then divide evenly between four bowls. Place the crispy-skinned barramundi on top and drizzle with a little olive oil.

After completing his apprenticeship at Claridge's Hotel, London, **Michael Lambie** worked at the Michelin two-star-rated Koenigshoff in Munich; the Waterside Inn, at Bray, in Berkshire, with Michel Roux; and with Marco Pierre White at Marco Pierre White, London. He established Circa at The Prince Hotel in Melbourne in 1998.

Circa, The Prince, 29 Fitzroy Street, St Kilda, Victoria 3182 (03 9536 1122); www.theprince.com.au

SERVES 4

12 cups vegetable stock
8 yabbies or small freshwater crayfish
4 sea scallops
2 carrots, diced
2 stalks celery, diced
1/2 cup olive oil
2 teaspoons saffron threads
16 mussels
16 clams
2 cups dry white wine
4 oysters
4 × 150 g (5 oz) fillets of wild barramundi
   or sea bass, skin on
4 tomatoes, cut into dice
1/2 cup chopped flat-leaf parsley
olive oil for drizzling

escabeche of shellfish with asparagus and citrus fruit

Liam Tomlin, Banc

You can use this technique for any seafood, such as fresh salmon, barramundi or swordfish – the vinegar in the escabeche marinade 'cooks' the fish. The yabbies and lobster are very briefly blanched in boiling water just to kill them before they are shelled. If you're feeling really generous you can serve this dish with caviar, as we do at Banc.

Place all the marinade ingredients except the saffron threads into a pan and bring to the boil. Reduce the heat and simmer gently until the shallots and fennel are cooked – about 7–10 minutes. Remove from the heat and allow the escabeche to cool.

Lay the shellfish in a deep dish and lightly season with salt and freshly ground pepper. Pour over the marinade and refrigerate for a couple of hours (the vinegar will 'cook' the shellfish, which will also become infused with the flavours of the marinade). Lift out the shellfish, pat dry with a clean cloth and arrange attractively on serving plates.

In a bowl, gently combine the citrus segments, asparagus and tomato. Season lightly with salt and pepper, then spoon over and around the shellfish.

Transfer 1 tablespoon of the escabeche marinade into a small pan and warm for a few minutes until the saffron threads release their flavour and colour, then pour back into the dish. Taste, adjust the seasoning and add a little more olive oil to thicken slightly, if needed. Pour over and around the shellfish. Garnish with mâche leaves.

Born in Ireland, **Liam Tomlin** began working in kitchens at the age of 14. He cooked at some of Europe's best addresses, and has done the same in Australia since arriving here in 1991, including stints at the Park Lane Hotel, Forty One and Brasserie Cassis. He is now chef and part-owner of Banc and Wine Banc.
Banc, 53 Martin Place, Sydney, New South Wales 2000 (02 9233 5300); www.banc.citysearch.com.au

SERVES 4

4 sea scallops
8 yabbies or freshwater crayfish,
    blanched and shelled
4 uncooked prawns (shrimp),
    cut in half lengthwise
4 Balmain bugs, shelled – optional
4 medallions of blanched and shelled lobster
8 pink grapefruit segments
8 orange segments
8 lime segments
8 asparagus spears, blanched
    and sliced on an angle
1 medium tomato, peeled and
    cut into large dice
salt and freshly ground black pepper
2 handfuls mâche leaves (lamb's lettuce)

MARINADE

1 teaspoon coriander seeds, crushed
2 golden shallots, finely sliced
1 baby fennel bulb, thinly sliced
finely grated zest of ½ lemon
finely grated zest and juice of ½ orange
1 tablespoon Pernod
3 tablespoons white wine vinegar
1 cup olive oil
pinch saffron threads

desserts

raspberry risotto with coconut ice-cream and a shard of bitter chocolate

David Danks

This sensational combination of fruit and chocolate flavours is a bit like a Cherry Ripe. The colours are beautiful and the flavours enticing.

To make the ice-cream, put milk and coconut milk in a pan, and bring to the boil. Cream egg yolks and sugar in a bowl, then add warm milk mixture and combine well. Pour into a clean pan and slowly cook over low heat, stirring constantly with a wooden spoon, until the mixture coats the back of the spoon. Strain through a sieve into a bowl, then set the bowl inside another bowl of iced water and whisk the custard until cool. Transfer to an ice-cream machine and churn according to manufacturer's instructions.

Place the coconut on a baking tray and toast in a 150°C (300°F) oven until lightly browned. Remove from oven and allow to cool.

Melt chocolate in a bowl set over a pan of barely simmering water until smooth. Line a baking tray with greaseproof paper and spread the melted chocolate over the paper. Chill in the refrigerator until set. Once hard, break the chocolate into shards.

Purée raspberries with 1 teaspoon of the caster sugar in a food processor or blender, then pass through a fine sieve.

Bring apple juice to the boil in a heavy-based stainless steel pan. Add rice and reduce heat to a simmer. Cook, stirring occasionally, until all the juice is absorbed. Pour risotto into a bowl and allow to cool for 5–10 minutes. Mix through raspberry purée and remaining caster sugar and refrigerate until chilled.

To serve, place a generous spoonful of risotto in each bowl. Top with a scoop of coconut ice-cream, stab a chocolate shard into the ice-cream and scatter with toasted coconut. Serve immediately.

David Danks moved to Australia from Glasgow in 1985, headed to London eight years later to work at Sir Terence Conran's mega-brasserie Quaglino's, then was head chef at Melbourne's highly respected Guernica until it closed in 2002.

SERVES 4

1 cup milk
3 cups coconut milk
12 egg yolks
250 g (8 oz) sugar
1/4 cup shredded coconut
100 g (3 1/2 oz) bitter chocolate
400 g (13 oz) fresh raspberries
5 teaspoons caster (superfine) sugar
1 3/4 cups apple juice
150 g (5 oz) arborio rice

cappuccino crème brûlée
Paul Wilson, the botanical

This was the first dish I created after coming to Melbourne; inspired by the city's coffee culture, it's a good all-round dessert.

Preheat oven to 110°C (230°F).

Place sugar, vanilla bean, cream and milk in a medium-sized pan. Whisk to dissolve sugar, bring to the boil and remove from heat. Add coffee extract and instant coffee, whisking until dissolved, then mix in egg yolks. Strain through a chinois or fine sieve.

Place six small coffee cups or ramekins in a deep baking tray. Using a jug, pour the mixture into the cups. Fill the baking tray with warm water to three-quarters of the way up the sides of the cups or ramekins. Bake for about 40 minutes, checking and carefully turning the tray after 30 minutes. When cooked, the crèmes should still be slightly wobbly.

Remove from oven and allow to cool in the water-filled tray. Refrigerate once cool. When chilled, sprinkle the top of each crème with a teaspoon of sugar. Caramelise the sugar by using a kitchen blowtorch or placing under a very hot grill.

For the sabayon, place Kahlua, water, egg yolks and caster sugar in a bowl. Half-fill a saucepan with cold water and place over low heat. Set the bowl over the top of the warming water and whisk the sabayon until light and frothy, taking care that it does not overheat and curdle. Remove from heat and continue whisking (by hand) for a further 8–10 minutes, until the sabayon becomes thick and creamy.

To serve, spoon sabayon on top of the crèmes, sprinkle with cocoa, decorate with coffee beans and serve with biscotti.

Paul Wilson was executive chef at Quaglino's in London before being lured to Melbourne by Terence Conran to help launch the new George's department store. He subsequently turned Radii, at the Park Hyatt Hotel, into one of the city's finest restaurants, and has recently relaunched Melbourne's landmark Botanical Hotel as a sleek modern brasserie called the botanical.

the botanical, 169 Domain Road, South Yarra, Victoria 3141 (03 9866 1684)

SERVES 6

75 g (2½ oz) caster (superfine) sugar
1 vanilla bean, split in half
300 ml (10 fl oz) whipping cream
¾ cup milk
2½ teaspoons coffee extract –
   Trablit is my preferred brand
2½ teaspoons instant coffee granules
9 egg yolks
6 teaspoons caster (superfine) sugar
cocoa powder for dusting
6 coffee beans, to garnish
biscotti, to serve

SABAYON
30 ml (1 fl oz) Kahlua
30 ml (1 fl oz) water
3 egg yolks
2 teaspoons caster (superfine) sugar

strawberry and vanilla trifles

Genevieve Harris

First, make the Swiss rolls. Preheat oven to 200°C (400°F) and line a Swiss roll tin – 30 × 20 cm (12 × 8 in) – with baking paper. Whisk eggs for about 7 minutes until light and fluffy. Gradually add sugar, still whisking. Gently fold in sifted flour, then milk. Spread one-third of mixture evenly onto the prepared tin. Bake for about 5 minutes. Meanwhile, spread out a clean tea towel on a benchtop and sprinkle caster sugar over it. Gently warm strawberry jam. When cake is cooked, turn out onto tea towel and cut in half to make two squares. Spread a thin layer of jam over each square, then quickly roll into a long roll. Repeat process with the other two-thirds of the Swiss roll mixture, in two batches. Set rolls aside.

For the vanilla cream, bring cream and vanilla bean to the boil in a stainless steel saucepan and allow to infuse off the heat for 15 minutes. In a heatproof bowl, whisk egg yolks and sugar until thick and creamy. Pour in cream, whisking continuously. Set bowl over a saucepan of barely simmering water and stir constantly until the vanilla cream is very thick. Strain through a fine sieve into a bowl, then stand bowl in iced water and whisk until cool. Set aside.

For the strawberry jelly, finely chop the 250 g (8 oz) of strawberries and place in a stainless steel saucepan with water, sugar and strawberry liqueur. Bring to the boil then remove from heat and allow to infuse for 1 hour. Bring back to the boil, then strain for 2–3 hours through a sieve lined with a coffee filter paper or muslin (cheesecloth), reserving strawberry pulp for later. Place strained strawberry liquid into a saucepan and warm gently. Soften gelatine leaves in cold water for 5 minutes then drain and squeeze out excess water. Place in strawberry liquid and stir to dissolve. Strain through a fine sieve and set aside to cool slightly.

To assemble trifles, slice Swiss rolls into rounds 1 cm (½ in) thick. Line bottom and sides of six trifle or tall beer glasses with slices of Swiss roll. Chop the 200 g (6 oz) of strawberries, toss in brandy and pile on top of cake. Gently spoon on a 2 cm (1 in) layer of vanilla cream. Whip cream, then fold in reserved strawberry pulp. Spoon a 2 cm (1 in) layer on top of vanilla cream. Carefully pour on a 2 cm (1 in) layer of jelly, and place trifles in refrigerator to set for at least 1 hour.

Genevieve Harris began her kitchen career in 1986 at her sister Marianne's restaurant, Grey Masts, at Robe, in South Australia. After cooking at several Sydney restaurants, she moved to Bali to take up the position of executive chef at Amankila resort, then returned to Sydney as executive chef of The Bathers' Pavilion. From 1997 to 2003, Genevieve and Marianne owned and ran Nediz restaurant in Adelaide. Genevieve is currently at Mount Lofty House, in the Adelaide Hills.

MAKES 6–8 INDIVIDUAL TRIFLES

200 g (6 oz) strawberries
50 ml (1½ fl oz) brandy
200 ml (6 fl oz) whipping cream

SWISS ROLLS
2 eggs
75 g (2½ oz) caster (superfine) sugar
75 g (2½ oz) self-raising flour, sifted
2 tablespoons milk
caster (superfine) sugar for dusting
1 large jar strawberry jam

VANILLA CREAM
375 ml (12 fl oz) cream
1 vanilla bean, split and seeds scraped out
6 egg yolks
75 g (2½ oz) caster (superfine) sugar

STRAWBERRY JELLY
250 g (8 oz) strawberries
150 ml (5 fl oz) water
50 g (1½ oz) caster (superfine) sugar
30 ml (1 fl oz) strawberry liqueur
2 gelatine leaves

chilled rice pudding with warm spiced pineapple

Barry Vera, Joseph's at The Mansion Hotel

I like using the traditional recipe for rice pudding and incorporating pineapple, which complements the star anise and vanilla flavours. It's perfect at any time of the year and can be served cold, as here, or warm . . . whatever your preference.

Put rice in a pan and cover with cold water. Bring to the boil then take off the heat and rinse under cold water. Transfer rice to a clean pan and add milk, cream, sugar and the deseeded vanilla bean. Simmer for about 45 minutes, but keep stirring or the starch from the rice will cause it to stick to the base of the pan. When the rice is cooked, transfer to a bowl and refrigerate for about 2 hours.

Melt butter in a pan, add pineapple, the split vanilla bean and star anise, and cook for 5 minutes. Add the rum, brown sugar and honey and cook for a further 5 minutes. Remove pineapple and reduce the liquid to a syrup. Remove syrup from heat and then stir the pineapple back in.

Take the chilled rice pudding from the fridge and stir through the 100 ml (3 fl oz) of cream. Divide evenly between six plates and place a spoonful of spiced pineapple in the centre of each. Drizzle a little of the syrup over and around the rice, and serve.

Sheffield-born **Barry Vera** conquered the London restaurant scene – Les Saveurs, Quaglino's, Quayside with Marco Pierre White, Cantina del Ponte and the Waldorf Hotel – before coming to Australia to assume the role of executive chef at The Mansion Hotel, just outside Melbourne.

Joseph's at The Mansion Hotel, Werribee Park, K Road, Victoria 3030 (03 9731 4130); www.mansionhotel.com.au

SERVES 6

100 g (3½ oz) short-grain rice
500 ml (16 fl oz) milk
500 ml (16 fl oz) cream
75 g (2½ oz) caster (superfine) sugar
1 vanilla bean, split and seeds scraped out
30 g (1 oz) unsalted butter
300 g (10 oz) fresh pineapple, diced
1 vanilla bean, split
1 star anise
30 ml (1 fl oz) dark rum
4 tablespoons brown sugar
2 tablespoons honey
100 ml (3 fl oz) cream, to serve

passionfruit pannacotta with poached pears, honey wafers and sauternes syrup

Stewart Wallace, Cafe Sydney

SERVES 4

100 ml (3 fl oz) white wine
200 ml (6 fl oz) water
200 g (6½ oz) caster (superfine) sugar
1 black peppercorn
1 star anise
½ cinnamon stick
2 honey, beurre bosc or corella pears
150 ml (5 fl oz) whipping cream
50 ml (1½ fl oz) honey

PANNACOTTA
300 ml (10 fl oz) cream
100 ml (3 fl oz) fresh passionfruit pulp,
    sieved – about 6–8 passionfruit
100 ml (3 fl oz) milk
100 g (3½ oz) caster (superfine) sugar
1 vanilla bean
1 gelatine leaf

HONEY WAFERS
250 g (8 oz) caster (superfine) sugar
200 g (6½ oz) plain (all-purpose) flour
325 g (10½ oz) butter
1 egg white
2 teaspoons honey

SYRUP
100 ml (3 fl oz) sauternes
100 ml (3 fl oz) water
100 g (3½ oz) caster (superfine) sugar

First, make the pannacotta. Put cream, passionfruit pulp, milk, sugar and vanilla into a saucepan and gently warm. Remove from heat just before it starts to boil. Soak gelatine in cold water until it starts to soften. Squeeze out excess water and add gelatine leaf to saucepan, stirring until it has dissolved completely. Pass the mixture through a sieve and skim off any fat that may appear. Allow to set slightly before pouring it into four pliable moulds. Let set overnight in refrigerator.

For the honey wafers, combine all ingredients in a food processor. Heat oven to 140°C (280°F) and line a baking sheet with non-stick baking paper. Take a teaspoon of the wafer mix and, using the back of the teaspoon, spread it out into a circle on the baking sheet. Repeat until you have twelve wafers. Bake for about 6 minutes, until crisp, then let cool. Remove from paper and store in an airtight container until ready to use.

To make the syrup, place sauternes, water and caster sugar in a saucepan, bring to a simmer and reduce liquid by a third, until it reaches a syrupy consistency.

For the poached pears, put white wine, water, sugar and spices in a pan and bring to the boil. Peel the pears and carefully lower into the poaching liquid. Cook for about 8–10 minutes, depending on the size of the pears – when they're ready, a knife should penetrate them easily. Remove from liquid and leave to cool. Slice in half, remove the core, then dice the flesh. Set aside.

Finally, whip the cream to soft peaks. Slightly warm the honey until it is about the same consistency as the cream – a microwave is perfect for this – then gently combine with the cream, being careful not to overwork.

To serve, spread a little cream on the wafers, top with diced pear, and place another wafer on top. Repeat the cream and pear layers, ending with a wafer. Unmould the pannacotta by dipping each mould in hot water for a few seconds, running a sharp knife around the inside of the top edge and inverting onto the centre of a plate. Place a wafer stack beside each pannacotta and drizzle with the sauternes syrup.

Stewart Wallace made a name for himself in Sydney at Fiorentino's and the Grand National before being lured to work at top restaurants in London and Cape Town. He returned home to become executive chef at Cafe Sydney in 2001.
Cafe Sydney, Fifth Floor, Customs House, Circular Quay, New South Wales 2000 (02 9251 8683); www.cafesydney.com

bread and butter puddings

Tracey Carroll, Lenzerheide Restaurant

SERVES 8

1 French stick (baguette)
100 g (3 oz) butter, melted
300 g (9 oz) caster (superfine) sugar
12 large eggs
4 cups milk
1¼ cups whipping cream
1 vanilla bean
50 g (1½ oz) sultanas
50 g (1½ oz) currants
2 tablespoons apricot jam, melted
fresh berries, to serve

VANILLA SAUCE

6 egg yolks
250 g (8 oz) caster (superfine) sugar
2 teaspoons vanilla essence
2 cups milk
2 cups whipping cream

These can be served either hot or cold. If you don't have time to make the vanilla sauce, simply serve with thick cream and fresh berries.

Cut the bread into slices 1 cm (½ in) thick. Butter each side of bread with melted butter, then arrange slices in a rosette pattern in eight buttered dariole or other cylindrical moulds. Place moulds inside a deep baking tray and preheat oven to 180°C (350°F).

Whisk sugar and eggs together. Place milk, cream and vanilla bean in a pan and bring to the boil. Pour milk mixture into eggs and sugar, whisk and strain (you can reserve the vanilla bean for future use), then pour into the moulds. Allow to soak into the bread before topping up the moulds again. Sprinkle with sultanas and currants. Fill the baking tray with warm water to come three-quarters of the way up the sides of the moulds. Bake for approximately 40 minutes, or until set.

Meanwhile, make the vanilla sauce. Whisk together egg yolks, sugar and vanilla essence until pale and fluffy. Combine milk and cream in a saucepan, and bring to the boil. Whisk this into the egg yolk mixture, then whisk the lot over a pan of barely simmering water until thick and frothy.

Remove puddings from oven and glaze with melted apricot jam while still warm. Allow puddings to cool for about 10 minutes then remove from moulds by running a knife around the inside and easing into serving bowls. Serve with the vanilla sauce and some fresh berries.

After completing her apprenticeship, **Tracey Carroll** was appointed executive chef at Lenzerheide Restaurant in 1989. The Lenzerheide has enjoyed considerable success during this period, winning numerous awards and gaining recognition as one of Adelaide's leading fine-dining establishments.
Lenzerheide Restaurant, 146 Belair Road, Hawthorn, South Australia 5062
(08 8373 3711); www.lenzerheide.com.au

lemongrass and palm sugar pannacotta with orange and chilli caramel

Don Cameron, Stillwater

My personal love of Asian food really shows in this dish. Combining a French technique with Asian produce, it is very pretty – and very sexy to eat. Liquid glucose, also known as light corn syrup, is available in most supermarkets.

To make the pannacotta, trim lemongrass and bruise with the back of the knife. Warm cream and milk in a saucepan, add caster sugar and palm sugar and stir until completely dissolved. Add lemongrass and simmer for 20 minutes, then boil briefly and remove from heat. Cover and set aside to allow the flavours to infuse.

Soak gelatine in cold water for 10 minutes, squeeze out excess water then add to pannacotta mixture and stir until completely dissolved. Let sit for 10 minutes, then strain through a sieve. Using a jug, pour into eight dariole moulds or ramekins and refrigerate for 4 hours, or until set.

For the orange and chilli caramel, make a simple sugar syrup by dissolving half of the sugar in 300 ml (10 fl oz) of hot water. Leave to cool. Dissolve the other half of the sugar and the glucose in 220 ml (7 fl oz) water over low heat. Add orange halves and continue to cook, swirling the pan (but trying not to let the sides get too sticky), until the mixture takes on a golden amber colour. Cool the pan in a bowl of tepid water. Remove orange halves and allow the caramel to cool completely before adding the finely chopped chilli. Blanch the slices of chilli and strips of orange zest twice in boiling water, then cook in the simple sugar syrup until chilli and zest are slightly translucent. Using a slotted spoon, remove candied chilli and orange from syrup and place on baking paper. When cool enough to handle, mould into eight red and orange clusters.

To serve, unmould the pannacotta with the help of a sharp, thin-bladed knife. Carefully invert a pannacotta onto the centre of each plate, then drizzle with the orange and chilli caramel. Pile candied chilli and orange on top and serve immediately.

Don Cameron was born and raised in north-western Tasmania but travels widely for culinary inspiration. Stillwater restaurant in Launceston, where he is chef and co-proprietor, has repeatedly been voted Tasmania's best – and was voted the Renault haute cuisine national restaurant of the year 2001/2002. **Stillwater**, Patterson Street, Launceston, Tasmania 7250 (03 6331 4153)

SERVES 8

PANNACOTTA
2 large stalks lemongrass
440 ml (14 fl oz) whipping cream
150 ml (5 fl oz) milk
45 g (1½ oz) caster (superfine) sugar
75 g (2½ oz) unprocessed palm sugar
2 leaves gelatine

CARAMEL
500 g (1 lb) caster (superfine) sugar
1 teaspoon liquid glucose (light corn syrup)
1 orange, cut in half
1 long red chilli, finely chopped and blanched
6 long red chillies, cut in half, deseeded and thinly sliced
zest of 1 orange, cut into thin strips

watermelon granita with melon pearls and noble one jelly

Yvan Meunier, Boathouse on Blackwattle Bay

Light and refreshing, this is perfect to finish a summer lunch – and is a great way to use the world-class melons grown in Australia.

Dice the watermelon flesh and blend in a food processor with the vodka and sugar. Strain through a coarse sieve, then pour into a shallow tray and freeze overnight.

Next day, soak the gelatine leaves in cold water for a few minutes until they soften. Pour half the dessert wine into a pan and bring to the boil. Take off the heat then add the remaining wine to the pan. Remove gelatine from water, squeezing out any excess liquid, then add to the wine, stirring to dissolve completely. Pour the wine jelly into four tumblers or cocktail glasses and place in fridge for a few hours to set.

When ready to serve, use a small round scoop or spoon to make 'pearls' from the honeydew and rockmelons. Pile the melon pearls into the glasses on top of the jelly. Remove watermelon granita from freezer, flake with a fork and place on top of melon pearls.

Raised in south-eastern France and inspired by his grandmother's traditional cooking, **Yvan Meunier** trained at France's premier hospitality school, Thonon Les Bains. He polished his craft at restaurants across Europe, worked in Sydney at the likes of Claude's and Merrony's, and has been head chef at the Boathouse on Blackwattle Bay, also in Sydney, since 1997.

Boathouse on Blackwattle Bay, End of Ferry Road, Glebe, New South Wales 2037 (02 9518 9011); www.bluewaterboathouse.com.au

SERVES 4

½ seedless watermelon – about 2 kg (4 lb)
60 ml (2 fl oz) vodka
60 g (2 oz) sugar
3 gelatine leaves
375 ml (12 fl oz) De Bortoli Noble One
   or any rich, sticky dessert wine
½ honeydew melon
½ rockmelon (cantaloupe)

Gold Coast, Queensland

Port Elliot, South Australia

figs in samos muscat

Peter Conistis

You can make the sorbet either in an ice-cream machine or granita-style, by freezing it on a tray and scraping the mix every half hour or so for a few hours.

For the sorbet, put sugar, water, lemon juice and glucose in a heavy-based stainless steel saucepan. Bring to the boil and simmer for 3 minutes. Cool, then place in a food processor with raspberries and rosewater. Process until smooth, then strain through a fine sieve. Churn in an ice-cream machine according to manufacturer's instructions. Alternatively, freeze on a tray, stirring every half hour or so for the first couple of hours.

Put all remaining ingredients except figs into a heavy-based stainless steel saucepan, bring to the boil and simmer for 5 minutes. Allow to cool. Pour over figs and chill until needed.

Serve the figs with a little of their syrup, a dash of muscat and a scoop of the sorbet.

Greek legend **Peter Conistis** operated Eleni's, in Sydney, for 10 years until early 2003. He has been an ambassador for Greek cuisine both in Australia and Greece, and has plans to open a new restaurant in the near future.

SERVES 6

150 ml (5 fl oz) Samos or other fine muscat
50 g (1½ oz) caster (superfine) sugar
2 tablespoons honey
1 vanilla bean, split open
finely grated zest and juice of 1 lemon
6 large black or green figs
a little extra muscat, to serve

RASPBERRY AND ROSE PETAL SORBET
150 g (5 oz) caster (superfine) sugar
300 ml (10 fl oz) water
3 tablespoons lemon juice
3 tablespoons liquid glucose (light corn syrup)
300 g (10 oz) raspberries
1 tablespoon rosewater

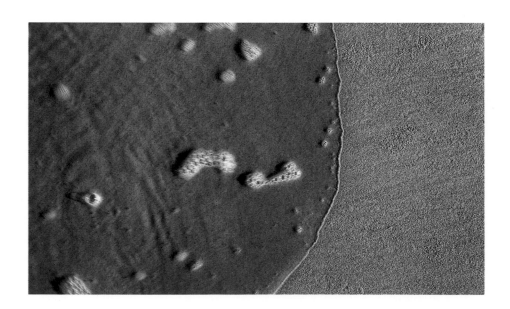

lemon, lime and cranberry chocolate meringue doorstop

Matthew Treloar, Windy Point Restaurant

SERVES 10

CHOCOLATE DOORSTOP

4 eggs

finely grated zest of ¼ orange

60 g (2 oz) caster (superfine) sugar

375 g (12 oz) dark couverture chocolate, melted

125 ml (4 fl oz) whipping cream, whisked to a stiff peak

LEMON CURD

3 egg yolks

75 g (2½ oz) caster (superfine) sugar

juice of 3 ripe lemons – about 75 ml (2½ fl oz)

75 g (2½ oz) unsalted butter, cubed

CRANBERRY CURD

3 egg yolks

75 g (2½ oz) caster (superfine) sugar

75 ml (2½ fl oz) cranberry juice

75 g (2½ oz) unsalted butter, cubed

LIME CURD

3 egg yolks

75 g (2½ oz) caster (superfine) sugar

juice of 3 ripe limes – about 75 ml (2½ fl oz)

75 g (2½ oz) unsalted butter, cubed

MERINGUE

4 egg whites

250 g (8 oz) icing (confectioner's) sugar

The chocolate doorstop part of this dessert can be made in advance – it will keep for 4–5 days. The curds can also be made a day or two in advance.

For the chocolate doorstop, preheat oven to 150°C (300°F). Line a 15 × 12 cm (6 × 5 in) cake tin with greaseproof paper and place a deep baking tray half-filled with water in the oven. Beat eggs, then add zest and sugar and heat over a water bath, stirring constantly, until it reaches a temperature of about 65°C (150°F) or is quite warm to the touch. Pour mixture into an electric mixer and whisk on high for 10–15 minutes. Turn mixer to low and gradually add melted chocolate. When fully combined, gently fold in the whipped cream. Transfer to the prepared cake tin, cover with foil and place in the baking tray of simmering water – the water level should be just below the rim of the cake tin. Bake for about 1 hour, or until set. Do not allow to rise – move down a shelf or decrease oven temperature by 20°C (70°F) if this starts to happen. Remove from oven and allow to cool overnight.

Make each curd separately using the same method: whisk egg yolks and sugar in a stainless steel bowl until creamy, then add juice and cubed butter. Heat by placing the bowl over a pan of simmering water, and stir constantly until thickened. Strain and allow to cool slightly before refrigerating.

When ready to serve, preheat oven to 240°C (500°F).

For the meringue, place egg whites in an electric mixer bowl and whisk on high until soft peaks form. Add sugar a little at a time, whisking continuously, until all sugar is added. Whisk for a further 2–3 minutes. The mixture should be firm, smooth and shiny.

Remove chocolate doorstop from tin and cut into 1 cm (½ in) slices. Lay the slices on a baking tray lined with non-stick baking paper and put in oven for 1–2 minutes. Remove tray from oven and transfer the slices to heatproof serving plates. Working quickly, spoon the three curds neatly onto each chocolate doorstop. Spoon the meringue mixture over and caramelise with a kitchen blowtorch or under a very hot grill until slightly browned.

Matthew Treloar has been cooking at home and abroad for more than 20 years. He is part-owner of the Windy Point Restaurant in South Australia, voted the state's best restaurant in 1999 and 2001.

Windy Point Restaurant, Windy Point Lookout, Belair Road, Belair, South Australia 5052 (08 8278 8255); www.windypointrestaurant.com.au

liquorice parfait with lime syrup
Luke Mangan, Salt

SERVES 6

50 g (1½ oz) liquorice
300 ml (10 fl oz) cream
2 eggs
1 egg yolk
60g (2 oz) sugar
2 teaspoons liquid glucose (light corn syrup)
2 tablespoons Pernod
lime segments, to garnish – optional

LIME SYRUP
250 g (8 oz) sugar
250 ml (8 fl oz) water
juice and finely grated zest of 1 lime

I love the yin and yang of this dish – the tartness of the lime cuts through the richness of the liquorice. It's a fantastic combination.

Place liquorice and cream in a small saucepan and heat gently without boiling until liquorice is very soft. Blend in a food processor until well combined, then strain through a fine sieve to remove the tiny pieces of liquorice. Set aside to cool.

In a small saucepan set inside a larger saucepan of gently simmering water, make a sabayon by whisking together eggs, egg yolk, sugar, glucose and Pernod until the mixture turns pale and fluffy. Remove from heat and continue whisking for 5 minutes as it cools. Fold half the sabayon into the liquorice mixture. Once combined, fold in the remaining sabayon. Pour into individual moulds or a log-shaped tin and freeze for at least 3 hours, preferably overnight.

For the lime syrup, bring sugar and water to the boil, stirring to ensure that the sugar dissolves. Remove from heat and add lime juice and zest to taste. Stir well and refrigerate.

To serve, lower the moulds or tin into hot water for a few seconds before carefully easing out the parfait. Either pour the lime syrup over, or serve it alongside in a jug. Garnish with lime segments, if desired.

Luke Mangan received his classical training from the likes of Hermann Schneider in Melbourne and Michel Roux in the UK. His first restaurant, Salt, quickly established its place among Sydney's best. He and business partner Lucy Allon also run Bistro Lulu and Moorish Restaurant and Bar, both in Sydney. **Salt**, 229 Darlinghurst Road, Darlinghurst, New South Wales 2010 (02 9332 2566); www.saltrestaurant.com.au

peach and almond tarts with crema di mascarpone

Philip Johnson, e'cco

You can substitute pears or apricots for the peaches in this recipe. It is always best to grind your own almonds, as a lot of the natural oil has already been lost in bought varieties – just whiz blanched almonds in a food processor.

Preheat oven to 180°C (350°F) and grease six individual tart tins, each about 10 cm (4 in) in diameter by 2.5 cm (1 in) deep.

Cut peaches into wedges, leaving skin on. Set aside.

In a bowl, combine the flour, ground almonds, the ½ cup of sugar and a pinch of salt. In another bowl, whisk together the olive oil, milk, cream, eggs and vanilla essence. Fold this mixture into the dry ingredients and pour into the prepared tart tins.

Randomly place peaches on top of the batter. Scatter over small knobs of butter, then sprinkle with the 2 tablespoons of caster sugar and the flaked almonds. Bake for 20–25 minutes, or until the tarts spring back when gently pressed.

To make the crema di mascarpone, lightly beat the mascarpone with a wooden spoon, add the egg yolks, icing sugar, lemon zest and vanilla scrapings and briefly beat again. The crema should have a thick, creamy consistency – add a little water if necessary.

Place the tarts on serving plates, dust liberally with icing sugar and serve with a generous spoonful of crema di mascarpone.

New Zealand-born **Philip Johnson** has been cooking for 25 years, including a stint working in London with Antony Worrall Thompson at dell'Ugo, and designing menus for Air New Zealand. He opened his Brisbane bistro, e'cco, in 1995 – and in 1997 it was named *Australian Gourmet Traveller* restaurant of the year.

e'cco, 100 Boundary Street, Brisbane, Queensland 4000 (07 3831 8344); www.eccobistro.com

SERVES 6

3 large, ripe but firm peaches –
   preferably freestone
1 cup self-raising flour
2 tablespoons ground almonds (almond meal)
½ cup caster (superfine) sugar
pinch salt
4 tablespoons olive oil
½ cup milk
½ cup cream
3 eggs
1 teaspoon vanilla essence
few knobs butter
2 tablespoons caster (superfine) sugar
⅓ cup flaked almonds
sifted icing (confectioner's) sugar, to serve

CREMA DI MASCARPONE
300 g (10 oz) mascarpone
2 egg yolks
½ cup icing (confectioner's) sugar, sifted
finely grated zest of 1 lemon
1 vanilla bean, scraped

vanilla and champagne sorbet

Janni Kyritsis

This is best made with good French champagne and served in martini glasses.

Place the sugar, water and vanilla bean in a saucepan and bring to the boil.

Allow to cool, then stir in 2 cups of the champagne. Keep the remaining champagne chilled.

Pour the mixture into an ice-cream machine and churn, according to the manufacturer's instructions, until firm.

To serve, place one rounded scoop of sorbet in a martini glass or similar. Take the sorbet to the table and pour over the remaining champagne in front of your guests.

Born in Greece and trained as an electrician, **Janni Kyritsis** got his first kitchen job – aged 30 – working for Stephanie Alexander, before moving to Sydney to work at Berowra Waters and Bennelong under Gay Bilson. His first restaurant, MG Garage, opened in Sydney in 1997 and became one of Australia's finest.

SERVES 6

3/4 cup caster (superfine) sugar
3/4 cup water
1 vanilla bean, split in half
1 bottle of champagne (preferably French), chilled

butterscotch ice-cream meringue cake

Rikki Jones, Blarney's by the Beach

SERVES 12

ICE-CREAM
300 g (9½ oz) soft brown sugar
125 g (4 oz) butter
300 g (9½ oz) golden syrup or corn syrup
5 cups whipping cream
12 egg yolks

MERINGUE
3 egg whites
350 g (11 oz) caster (superfine) sugar
pinch cream of tartar
1 teaspoon cornflour (cornstarch)

This cake can be prepared in advance, ready for when friends arrive.

Preheat oven to very low – about 55°C (130°F).

Place all meringue ingredients in an electric mixer and whisk on medium speed until meringue starts to form, then increase to high speed until thick and glossy. Using the loose base of a 20 cm (8 in) springform cake tin as a template, draw two circles on non-stick baking paper. Place the paper on a baking tray and spoon meringue evenly within each circle, keeping 1 cm (½ in) inside the edges. The meringues should stand about 2 cm (1 in) high – you may not need to use all the mixture. Place meringue circles in oven for 8–10 hours, until very firm and dry. Remove from paper and store in an airtight container.

Cook brown sugar, butter, syrup and 1 cup of the cream in a saucepan over medium heat, stirring occasionally, until all ingredients have melted together and formed a butterscotch sauce. Boil for 1–2 minutes, then turn off heat.

Place egg yolks in a food processor on high, adding the hot butterscotch in a steady stream – this will cook the yolks. Transfer the mixture to a large mixing bowl and pour in the remaining 4 cups of cream. Whisk until thoroughly combined. If making the ice-cream by hand, place in the freezer for 24 hours, stirring every few hours to break up the ice crystals as they form. When the ice-cream is firm but not too solid, beat in an electric mixer with a beater attachment for 30–40 seconds, until light and fluffy but still firm. If using an ice-cream machine, follow manufacturer's instructions.

Working as quickly as possible, put one-third of the ice-cream in a 20 cm (8 in) chilled springform cake tin and top with one of the meringues. Add another third of the ice-cream, followed by the second meringue, then top with the remaining ice-cream. Place in the freezer for 12 hours, then invert onto a polyurethane cutting board that has been chilled in the freezer for 2 hours. Remove the cake tin by running warm hands over it or using a kitchen blowtorch to warm it. Return the ice-cream cake to the freezer to firm up, then use a hot knife to cut into slices. Serve immediately.

Rikki Jones arrived in Queensland from England in 1991, via cooking stints in Saudi Arabia, Bermuda, Switzerland and the Channel Islands. Blarney's is his second restaurant at Mission Beach, and he runs it with his wife, Angela, and their children.
Blarney's by the Beach, 10 Wongaling Beach Road, Mission Beach, Queensland 4852 (07 4068 8472)

chinese five-spice soufflé with poached nashi pears

Fiona Hoskin, Fee and Me

The fail-safe soufflé? Have the eggs at room temperature, be gentle but quick when folding in the egg whites, don't let the mixture touch the rims when spooning it into the soufflé dishes (or the soufflés will rise unevenly), and cook them immediately.

Peel, core and dice the nashi pears. Bring the wine and the 100 g (3 oz) sugar to the boil in a stainless steel pan then add the nashi and poach for 5 minutes. Remove from heat but leave the fruit in the poaching liquid to absorb the flavour.

Melt the 125 g (4 oz) of butter in a saucepan, then add the flour and cook gently for 5 minutes, stirring so the mixture doesn't brown or catch on the bottom. Add the 225 g (7 oz) sugar and the milk and stir with a wooden spoon until the mixture reaches boiling point and is very thick and smooth. Set aside to cool while you grease eight soufflé dishes with soft (not melted) butter, then coat them evenly with caster sugar. Add the egg yolks to soufflé mixture, along with the five-spice powder, and stir thoroughly.

Preheat oven to 180°C (350°F). Whip the egg whites until they just hold their peaks, then stir 1 tablespoon of egg white into the soufflé mixture. Quickly but gently fold in the rest of the egg whites, then carefully spoon the mixture into the soufflé dishes until they are three-quarters full. Place on a baking sheet and bake for 25 minutes.

Serve immediately with the poached nashi and plenty of thick cream.

New Zealand-born **Fiona Hoskin** has lived in Tasmania for 20 years and is passionate about the island state's food and climate, insisting that she wouldn't want to be cooking anywhere else in the world. Fee and Me opened in 1989 and has won many national and state awards.

Fee and Me, 190 Charles Street, Launceston, Tasmania 7250 (03 6331 3195); www.feeandme.com.au

SERVES 8

2 nashi pears
¼ cup white wine
100 g (3 oz) sugar
125 g (4 oz) butter
125 g (4 oz) plain (all-purpose) flour
225 g (7 oz) sugar
2 cups milk
softened butter for greasing soufflé dishes
caster (superfine) sugar for coating
    soufflé dishes
6 eggs, separated
2 teaspoons Chinese five-spice powder
thick cream, to serve

Tamar River, Tasmania

fruit salad with kaffir lime leaves

Bruno Loubet, Bruno's Table

The exotic taste of kaffir lime complements the fresh flavours of fruit salad. This dessert is particularly good topped with a scoop of passionfruit sorbet.

Slice the tops and bottoms off the oranges and cut away all the pith and skin. Working over a bowl, cut either side of the segments to release them from the membranes. Add all the other fruit to the bowl and sprinkle with the 5 tablespoons of sugar. Add lime juice and leave to marinate for 1 hour, mixing from time to time.

Bruise the kaffir lime leaves on a chopping board with the back of a spoon. In a small saucepan, combine the water with the 2 tablespoons of sugar, the lime zest and kaffir lime leaves, and boil for 5 minutes. Remove from heat and allow to cool slightly. Soak the gelatine in cold water for a few minutes to soften. Squeeze out excess water and add the gelatine to the warm syrup, stirring until completely dissolved. Pass this jelly mixture through a fine sieve into a bowl, then refrigerate until set.

To serve, spoon the jelly into the fruit salad, mix well and divide between four bowls.

In 2001, **Bruno Loubet** left a stellar career in the UK – Le Manoir aux Quat' Saisons, Le Petit Blanc, L'Odeon, Isola, Four Seasons Mayfair – for Queensland, to open the highly regarded Bruno's Table and enjoy a far less hectic life.
Bruno's Table, 85 Miskin Street, Toowong, Queensland 4066 (07 3371 4558)

SERVES 4

2 oranges
¼ pineapple, cut into chunks
4 kiwi fruit, sliced
2 mangoes, diced
1 banana, sliced
150 g (5 oz) watermelon flesh,
    cut into chunks
10 strawberries, cut into quarters
5 tablespoons caster (superfine) sugar
juice of 1 lime
4 kaffir lime leaves
¾ cup water
2 tablespoons caster (superfine) sugar
finely grated zest of 1 lime
1 gelatine leaf

fresh cheese soufflé with lime sauce

Thomas Clever, On the Inlet

SERVES 4

90 g (3 oz) sugar
7 egg whites
½ teaspoon finely grated lime zest
½ teaspoon finely grated lemon zest
100 g (3½ oz) fresh cheese – quark is ideal
softened butter for greasing soufflé moulds
caster (superfine) sugar for coating
    soufflé moulds
thin slices of lime and slivers of lemon zest,
    to garnish

SAUCE
75 g (2½ oz) sugar
juice of 2 limes
200 ml (6½ fl oz) white wine
finely grated zest of 3 limes
1 tablespoon finely grated ginger

This is a fairly light dessert, with a tropical kick thanks to the lime and ginger.

Preheat oven to 180°C (350°F). Whisk half of the sugar with three of the egg whites and the lime and lemon zest until creamy. Add the fresh cheese and whisk until all ingredients are combined. Whisk the remaining four egg whites and the rest of the sugar until the mixture just holds its peaks, then carefully fold the cheese mixture through.

Grease five soufflé moulds with a little softened butter and sprinkle some sugar inside the moulds. Three-quarters fill moulds with the soufflé mixture. Pour boiling water into a deep baking tray to a depth of 3 cm (about 1 in). Place the soufflés in the tray of water and bake for 15–20 minutes.

Meanwhile, make the lime sauce. In a saucepan over medium heat, lightly caramelise the sugar. When it turns a light golden brown, add the lime juice, wine, lime zest and ginger. Reduce a little until the sauce thickens.

To serve, pour some lime sauce around the edge of each plate, carefully unmould a soufflé and place in the middle. Garnish with thinly sliced lime and slivers of lemon zest.

Originally from Germany, **Thomas Clever** worked in Michelin two- and three-star restaurants across Europe, including with the Roux brothers in London, before moving south to the sun in 1998. He has been executive chef at On the Inlet, in Port Douglas, Queensland, since 2000.
On the Inlet, 3 Inlet Street, Port Douglas, Queensland 4871 (07 4099 5255)

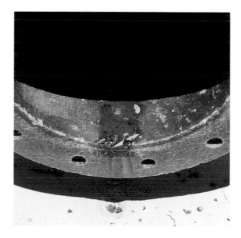

summer berries with champagne syllabub and basil ice-cream

Owen Lacey, Circa

The ice-cream is best prepared the day before, so it can set properly.

To make the syllabub, simmer the champagne in a pan over medium heat until reduced by three-quarters. Allow to cool, then add to the cream in a bowl. Whisk, gradually pouring in lemon juice as the mixture thickens.

For the ice-cream, boil together the 100 g (3½ oz) sugar and the water until sugar dissolves. Allow to cool. Blanch basil leaves in boiling water for 5–10 seconds, until bright green. Remove and refresh in iced water. Drain well, roughly chop, and place in blender with the cooled sugar syrup. Strain the liquid onto the slightly softened vanilla ice-cream, stir through well and return ice-cream to freezer to set.

Place berries in a stainless steel bowl, sprinkle with the 2 tablespoons of sugar then tightly wrap the bowl in cling film. Sit the bowl on top of a saucepan of barely simmering water over minimum heat for 30 minutes, to soften and warm the berries.

To serve, place a scoop of basil ice-cream in the centre of each plate, scatter the berries around, pour some berry juice over the ice-cream and dollop syllabub about the plate.

Owen Lacey was born in Canada, raised in New Zealand, and has cooked in Australia at various five-star resorts, including the Brisbane Treasury Casino and Ayers Rock. He is currently executive chef at Circa in Brisbane.
Circa, 483 Adelaide Street, Brisbane, Queensland 4000 (07 3832 4722); www.circarestaurant.com.au

SERVES 4–6

200 ml (7 fl oz) champagne
180 ml (6 fl oz) whipping cream
juice of 1 lemon
100 g (3½ oz) caster (superfine) sugar
150 ml (5 fl oz) water
¼ cup chopped basil leaves, or to taste
1½ cups vanilla ice-cream, slightly softened by placing in refrigerator for 30 minutes
2½ cups mixed berries, such as strawberries, raspberries and blueberries
2 tablespoons caster (superfine) sugar

blood orange, tangelo and mint salad

Matthew Kemp, Restaurant Balzac

Ideally this dessert should be eaten as soon as it is made, when the granita is at its lightest and most summery. You can leave the granita overnight, but it will crystallise a bit more.

Peel and segment half the fruit over a bowl to catch the juices. Juice the remaining fruit, then pass all the juices through a fine sieve and set aside.

In a saucepan, bring the sugar and water to the boil, stirring until the sugar dissolves and starts to form a syrup (this should take only a few minutes). Remove from the heat and allow to cool.

Whisk the cooled syrup with 2 cups of the reserved fruit juices, then pour into a shallow metal or plastic tray. Place tray in freezer, but scrape the mixture with a fork every 30–45 minutes for about 4 hours, to break up the ice crystals and create a granita.

To serve, cut the mint leaves into fine strips and mix with the fruit segments. Place a layer of granita in the bottom of each of four tall glass. Top with a layer of fruit segments and mint, then repeat these layers until the glasses are full. Garnish with sprigs of mint.

Matthew Kemp has wanted to be a cook since he was 11. His mother, a waitress, secured him an apprenticeship in London at a suitable age, and he has since worked with the likes of Dietmar Sawyere, Liam Tomlin and Phillip Howard. His cooking is driven by seasonality, using the freshest produce available.

Restaurant Balzac, 38–40 St Pauls Street, Randwick, New South Wales 2031 (02 9399 9660)

SERVES 4

10 blood oranges
10 large tangelos
100 g (3½ oz) caster (superfine) sugar
100 ml (3 fl oz) water
½ cup mint leaves – ideally spearmint
small sprigs of mint, to garnish

pavlova with rhubarb and lime

John Schirmer, The Queenscliff Hotel

Pavlova is the great Australian dessert. I've tried a lot of recipes and this one seems to work the best. It's very simple – and you really can't find a better pav.

Preheat oven to 200°C (400°F). Wash rhubarb thoroughly, remove leaves and chop stalks into 2 cm (1 in) batons. Place in a baking dish and cover with orange juice and the teaspoon of sugar. Bake for 8 minutes, or until the rhubarb has softened but not disintegrated. Remove and set aside, then lower the oven temperature to 160°C (325°F), ready for the meringues.

To make the meringues, place egg whites, caster sugar, vinegar, cornflour, warm water and vanilla essence in a mixing bowl and whisk in a cake mixer on high for 6 minutes, or until firm peaks form.

Line a baking tray with baking paper and, using a piping bag, pipe some meringue into a circle about 4 cm (1½ in) in diameter. Keep piping in a spiral formation until the sides of the meringue are about 4 cm (1½ in) high – they will puff up in the oven to nearly double the size. Repeat this process for the other three pavlovas.

Bake the meringues at 160°C (325°F) for about 10 minutes, then reduce the oven temperature to 100°C (210°F) and bake for a further 20 minutes.

Meanwhile, whip the cream until soft peaks form. Slowly fold through the lime juice and zest, being careful that the cream doesn't curdle.

When cooked, place a meringue on each of four plates, spoon lime cream into the centre and top with rhubarb. Drizzle with the rhubarb juices.

John Schirmer did his apprenticeship in Melbourne at the Stokehouse with Michael Lambie, worked at the venerable Lynch's in South Yarra, and at Langton's with Philippe Mouchel. He became head chef at The Queenscliff Hotel, on the Bellarine Peninsula, southwest of Melbourne, in 2002.
The Queenscliff Hotel, 16 Gellibrand Street, Queenscliff, Victoria 3225 (03 5258 1066); www.queenscliffhotel.com.au

SERVES 4

3 stalks rhubarb
about 2 cups orange juice
1 teaspoon sugar
4 egg whites
220 g (7 oz) caster (superfine) sugar
1 teaspoon white vinegar
pinch cornflour (cornstarch)
1 teaspoon warm water
drop of vanilla essence
2 cups whipping cream
juice and finely grated zest of 1 lime

Bellarine Peninsula, Victoria

hot chocolate puddings with a pistachio heart

Vincent Bonnin, C Restaurant

SERVES 10

250 g (8 oz) dark couverture chocolate
   (50% cocoa mass)
250 g (8 oz) unsalted butter
200 g (6½ oz) plain (all-purpose) flour
185 g (6 oz) caster (superfine) sugar
1 level teaspoon baking powder
8 large eggs
100 g (3½ oz) white couverture chocolate
75 ml (2½ fl oz) whipping cream
30 g (1 oz) pistachio paste
softened unsalted butter for greasing
   metal rings or ramekins
icing (confectioner's) sugar for dusting

Most of this dessert has to be made the day before you serve it, but it's well worth the effort. Serve with a dollop of mascarpone or a scoop of good-quality vanilla ice-cream. Pistachio paste is available in select delicatessens; if you can't find it, blanch a handful of pistachio nuts in boiling water for 5 minutes, then drain and blend or crush into a paste.

For the chocolate puddings, bring a large saucepan half full of water to the boil, then reduce to a simmer. Chop dark chocolate and butter into pieces and place in a large, heatproof bowl. Place this on top of the saucepan, and stir with a wooden spoon every 5 minutes until completely melted. Remove from the heat.

Meanwhile, sift flour, caster sugar and baking powder into a large bowl. Make a well in the centre, break in eggs and whisk into a paste. Pour this over the melted chocolate and butter and whisk until smooth – pass the mixture through a fine sieve if you find any lumps. Cover with cling film and refrigerate overnight.

For the pistachio heart, bring a medium-sized saucepan half full of water to the boil, then reduce to a simmer. Chop white chocolate, combine with cream and pistachio paste in a medium-sized bowl, and place over the saucepan. Stir with a wooden spoon until melted. Take the bowl off the heat and leave to cool. Cover with cling film and refrigerate overnight. Grease ten metal rings or ramekins – about 5 cm (2 in) in diameter – with butter and refrigerate overnight.

The next day, preheat oven to 220°C (450°F). Line a baking tray with greaseproof paper, place chilled rings or ramekins on top and spoon or pipe in the chocolate mixture until half full. Add a teaspoon of pistachio mixture to the middle of each pudding, then cover with remaining chocolate mixture. Bake for 10 minutes. Remove from oven and allow to cool for 2 minutes. Place puddings on individual plates and remove ring or ramekin (loosen with a knife if necessary). Dust with icing sugar and serve immediately, with mascarpone or vanilla ice-cream on the side.

Born in Le Mans, France, **Vincent Bonnin** has worked in some fine kitchens in Provence and regional England and, lately, in Australia – with Alain Fabrègues at The Loose Box, and at Altos Restaurant in Perth.

C Restaurant, Level 33, St Martin's Tower, 44 St Georges Terrace, Perth, Western Australia 6000 (08 9220 8333)

vacherin of roasted figs and vanilla bean ice-cream with blueberries in red wine and star anise syrup

Philippa Sibley-Cooke, Ondine

The crunch of meringue, the warm fruit and cold ice-cream, the affinity of vanilla with berries and figs – this dessert has got it all.

Simmer all syrup ingredients except blueberries for 15 minutes, then remove from heat and allow to infuse for a further 15 minutes. Bring back to the boil, then strain syrup over blueberries. Set aside. (This can be prepared a day in advance and refrigerated until needed.)

For the ice-cream, split and scrape the seeds from the vanilla beans and add both seeds and pods to the milk. Bring to the boil and remove from the heat. Whisk sugar into egg yolks until pale and light. Whisk in hot vanilla milk and return to the heat. Stir with a wooden spoon over moderate heat until the mixture thickens enough to coat the spoon. Remove from the heat and strain into a bowl, preferably a metal one. Set aside. (The ice-cream can also be made a day in advance up to this stage and refrigerated overnight.) When completely cool, add the cream. Churn in an ice-cream machine for no more than 1–2 hours.

For the meringue, preheat oven to 100°C (210°F) and line a heavy baking sheet with non-stick baking paper. In an electric mixer, whisk the egg whites with half the icing sugar until firm, then beat in the remaining sugar and continue to whisk until the mixture is stiff and shiny. Use a piping bag to pipe the meringue onto the paper-lined baking sheet in six of the desired shape. Bake for 1 hour 50 minutes. Allow to cool, then peel off the paper.

Peel the figs and cut in half lengthways. Sprinkle with sugar and put under a hot grill until bubbling. Allow to cool slightly.

To serve, put a meringue on each plate and arrange four half figs on top. Put the ice-cream into a piping bag with a star nozzle and pipe decoratively over the figs, making sure they are still visible underneath. Place another meringue on top. Arrange some berries around the vacherin and spoon around some syrup. Serve immediately.

Philippa Sibley-Cooke arrived in London a novice, landed a job at Harvey's with Pierre Marco White, then worked at some of the city's biggest names: Canteen, Quaglino's, Le Gavroche. In 2002 she and partner Donovan Cooke opened Ondine, the successor to their landmark Melbourne restaurant, est est est.

Ondine, 299 Queen Street, Melbourne, Victoria 3000 (03 9602 3477); www.ondine.com.au

---

SERVES 6

12 perfect fresh figs
sugar for sprinkling

SYRUP
½ bottle good red wine – cabernet gives the syrup a lovely colour
zest of ½ orange
½ vanilla bean
3 star anise
200 g (6½ oz) sugar
1 punnet blueberries – about 125 g (4 oz)

ICE-CREAM
2 vanilla beans
500 ml (16 fl oz) milk
125 g (4 oz) caster (superfine) sugar
6 egg yolks
100 ml (3 fl oz) cream

MERINGUE
3 large egg whites
185 g (6 oz) icing (confectioner's) sugar, sifted

Star of Greece Café, Port Willunga, South Australia

index

Italic type indicates names of restaurants.